SCIENCE FICTION WRITING 101

How To Write And Publish Your First Novel - Fast!

HACKNEY AND JONES

Contents

Foreword

We are Claire and Vicky from **Hackney and Jones Publishing**.
Together, we have created, written, and published hundreds of
fiction and non-fiction books and have learned a fair bit along the
exciting journey that is book publishing.

From our extensive experience in this field, we understand how difficult writing can be, whether it's fiction or non-fiction - which is why
we're here to provide assistance.

Believe us, we've made our fair share of mistakes along the way.
We've learned from them and now want to help you avoid them.
That's why we've done all the research and hard work so you don't
have to.

We know what it takes to craft an engaging book, and we want to
share that expertise with you here.

But more than just experience, our passion is what drives us
forward. Everyone has an important narrative to tell, so let us help
you tell it in the best way possible.

Writing can be a lonely pursuit, but it doesn't have to be. With our support, you'll have an objective guide and an encouraging friend at your side that will cheer you on as you reach success. Let us encourage and motivate you toward your objectives!

We believe in the power of stories to transform lives, to make us laugh or cry, and to inspire and challenge us - and we want to assist you with telling your own unique narrative.

We invite you to join us on this exciting journey. Whether you're an experienced writer or just starting out, our support and guidance can make the process smooth and turn your writing goals into reality.

Let's do this!

The Key Elements Of A
Science Fiction Novel

Science fiction is a genre that explores imaginative, futuristic concepts with a scientific or technological basis. Below are the key components of a good science fiction novel and examples:

Sci-fi novels often introduce innovative and imaginative concepts, including time travel, interstellar travel, and advanced artificial intelligence. H. G. Wells explored time travel in his novel, **"The Time Machine,"** while Douglas Adams' **"Hitchhiker's Guide to the Galaxy"** introduced interstellar travel and alternate universes.

Science fiction often features futuristic technology that does not yet exist in our everyday world, such as robots, cyborgs, and advanced weapons. Isaac Asimov's **"I, Robot"** features robots with human-like intelligence; William Gibson's **"Neuromancer"** offers cyberspace and virtual reality features.

Futuristic settings: Science fiction novels often take place in either an alternate or futuristic version of our world, like Aldous Huxley's **"Brave New World,"** which depicts an oppressive dystopian society; or on another planet entirely, like Frank Herbert's **"Dune"**, with its own ecosystem and political system.

Scientific accuracy: Although science fiction often contains fictional elements, many authors strive to include real science and technology in their stories. Andy Weir's novel **"The Martian"** draws heavily upon real scientific principles to explore how an astronaut might survive on Mars using only their knowledge and resourcefulness if stranded there.

Social and political commentary: Science fiction frequently examines social and political issues through futuristic worlds and technology, such as **"The Handmaid's Tale"** by Margaret Atwood, who examines patriarchy, and Neal Stephenson's **"Snow Crash,"** which discusses corporate power within society.

These are only some examples of what makes a successful science fiction novel, though its possibilities are virtually limitless.

Common questions about the elements that make up a science fiction novel

Q. How do science fiction authors create believable futuristic worlds?

A. Science fiction writers must craft convincing future worlds, which can be accomplished using several strategies:

Research: Science fiction authors often conduct extensive research to ensure their futuristic world reflects scientific principles and technology, which may include studying current research as well as exploring historical or cultural influences that may impact it in some way.

World-building: World-building is one of the primary steps in creating a believable futuristic world, comprising creating an intricate yet immersive setting, shaping it so it feels real and consistent across geography, climate, culture, politics, and technology.

Consistency: A convincing futuristic world must adhere to certain logical standards. Any technology or scientific concepts introduced should make sense and progress naturally through the story.

Character perspective: Character perspectives can also contribute to making futuristic worlds seem believable; their attitudes, beliefs and experiences help give more substance and depth to it all.

Balancing familiarity and uniqueness: For any futuristic world to succeed, readers need to feel they can relate to it while finding its contents intriguing and unique. A successful futuristic setting should find this balance.

Q. What role do science and technology play in science fiction novels?

A. Science and technology play an integral part in science fiction novels, shaping stories and themes explored by authors. Here are a few ways science and technology feature:

Exploration and speculation: Science fiction often explores the potential of new and developing scientific theories and technologies, offering speculation as to their development and impact on society in the future.

Critique and commentary: Science fiction can serve as a powerful medium for social and political commentary, with technological developments serving as metaphors for real-life conflicts and issues.

Science fiction authors use scientific and technological advancements to craft intricate yet plausible future worlds, often featuring inventions or discoveries that change the environment, culture, and society of these futuristic settings.

Problem solved by science & technology: Science and technology often play an essential role in solving problems found within science fiction novels, whether they involve medical emergencies, natural disasters, or technological malfunctions.

Conflict and consequences: Science fiction can explore advances that create conflict and consequences, whether that means creating new weapons of mass destruction or societies that have lost touch with their humanity.

Q. How do science fiction authors create compelling characters in futuristic settings?

A. Generating engaging characters is an integral aspect of fiction writing in all genres, including science fiction.

Here are some ways that science fiction authors create captivating and memorable characters set in futuristic settings:

Relatable emotions: Although science fiction takes place in alternate universes, its characters still must possess emotions and motivations that resonate with readers and create empathy among their audience.

Science fiction characters often possess distinct physical or mental characteristics that distinguish them from humans, such as telepathy or cybernetic implants. These unique traits add an extra dimension and depth to their characters while altering how they interact with the surrounding environment.

Science fiction often explores themes of identity and what it means to be human, using characters who question their own identities or interact with nonhuman characters as vehicles for exploring these ideas.

Q. How do science fiction authors balance scientific accuracy with storytelling?

Science fiction authors often strive to strike an appropriate balance between scientific accuracy and storytelling in their stories to produce engaging tales with realistic realism. Here are some ways they do so:

Research: Science fiction authors often undertake extensive research to ensure their stories contain plausible scientific concepts and technology, consulting experts from relevant fields or reviewing scientific literature as part of this process.

Simplification: Authors often must simplify complex scientific concepts to make them more easily understandable by readers without compromising accuracy. This may involve breaking complex ideas down into simpler ones or employing analogies as a way of explaining them.

Creative liberties: While authors strive for scientific accuracy, they may take creative liberties to enhance storytelling. This may involve inventing new scientific concepts or extrapolating existing ones in unexpected ways.

Focus on characters: Science fiction stories often revolve around characters' experiences rather than solely the scientific concepts or technology at hand. By emphasising how characters react to them, authors can produce more emotionally engaging narratives.

Suspension of disbelief: Readers of science fiction suspend their disbelief in favour of an engaging tale, so authors can add futuristic technologies or concepts as long as they fit within the story and remain internally consistent and make sense within the context.

Q. What is the importance of world-building in science fiction novels?

World-building is an integral component of science fiction writing, providing the setting and context for the story to take place. Here are a few reasons world-building matters when writing science fiction novels:

Immersion: World-building allows readers to step inside a detailed and believable environment as part of the story, immersing themselves completely and feeling part of that world.

Suspension of disbelief: World-building can be used to suspend disbelief in a fictional world and make stories more believable and captivating for readers. By building a consistent and logical universe for their story to inhabit, readers are more likely to accept any fantastical elements found within it.

Context: World-building provides context for the characters and their experiences. By creating an understanding of the geography, history, and culture within which these experiences take place, readers are better equipped to comprehend the motivations behind the decisions and choices made by characters.

Exploration of themes: World-building can explore themes and concepts relevant to a story's plot line, such as dystopias that explore authoritarianism or advanced technology environments that show unchecked technological growth.

World-building allows authors to craft original settings not found elsewhere, creating more engaging and memorable stories for their audience.

World-building is an essential aspect of science fiction writing that allows authors to craft compelling and believable narratives. By creating an expansive yet cohesive world, authors can explore themes and ideas specific to the science fiction genre.

Q. How do science fiction authors explore social and political issues through their writing?

Science fiction authors often use their writing to examine social and political issues through futuristic or speculative worlds. Here are a few ways they do this:

Metaphors: Science fiction authors use metaphors as a way of exploring social and political issues in their stories, such as how dystopian societies may expose authoritarianism's dangers, while genetically modified humans present unique challenges regarding discrimination and inequality.

Eg.

"The Hunger Games" by Suzanne Collins is an excellent science fiction novel that uses metaphors to explore social and political issues.

Set in a dystopian society where the wealthy Capitol oppresses impoverished districts by forcing them into an annual televised fight-to-the-death tournament known as The Hunger Games, its metaphor serves as a commentary on social inequality, government control, media power, sacrifice, rebellion, and corruption of power. **"The Hunger Games"** serves as a powerful critique of contemporary society and politics through its powerful use of metaphors and futuristic world-building.

Critique of current society: Science fiction writers often use writing as a platform to comment on our society through sci-fi writing. By creating worlds that differ drastically from our own, science fiction authors can highlight flaws and problems within society that may otherwise remain unseen.

Exploration of human nature: Science fiction can be used as an avenue to examine some of the darker sides of humanity, such as greed, power, and control. By creating a different world from our own, authors can draw attention to these issues in a more abstract and thought-provoking manner.

Science fiction authors explore the future: Science fiction authors often speculate on how scientific and technological advancements will shape society in the future, including issues like climate change, artificial intelligence, and genetic engineering. This includes looking into issues like climate change, artificial intelligence, and genomic engineering.

Overall, science fiction writers use their writing to explore social and political issues through a uniquely scientific lens. By envisioning alternative worlds to our own, science fiction authors can highlight flaws in our current society as well as provide thought-provoking perspectives about humanity's future.

2

How Do Science Fiction Writers Make Money?

Science fiction writers can make money in several ways, including:

Book sales: Writing and publishing science fiction novels is the primary means by which authors make money. Both physical and digital sales of their works generate royalties. Audio versions may also bring in profits for authors.

The royalty rate and calculation method can depend on both your publisher and contract terms, though royalties are determined based on net sales of your book or revenue generated minus any discounts, returns, or deductions (such as refunds).

Royalty rates can differ widely depending on the publisher and contract terms, but traditionally published works typically offer royalty rates between 6–10% of the retail price for print editions and 20–25% of net sales for digital editions.

Royalty payments typically arrive either quarterly or biannually by check or direct deposit.

Authors have every right to negotiate the rates they receive from publishers; however, be aware that publishers may be reluctant to offer higher royalty rates to new or unestablished authors.

Movie or TV deals: Popular science fiction books can easily be adapted into movies or TV shows, allowing authors to sell the rights for a substantial fee and receive royalties upon their success.

Merchandising: Successful science fiction books can be turned into merchandise like posters, t-shirts, and action figures, providing authors with an avenue for royalties by licensing their intellectual property to companies that create the merchandise.

Video games: Authors can earn money by licensing their intellectual property or creating the story and dialogue of a video game adaptation of their science fiction book.

Public speaking: Renowned science fiction authors can make money speaking at events, conventions, or schools for a fee for their time and expertise.

Crowdfunding: Some science fiction authors use crowdfunding platforms like Kickstarter to raise money for their book projects. Fans can contribute funds in exchange for special rewards such as signed copies or merchandise from the author.

Patreon: Some science fiction authors use Patreon as a membership platform that allows fans to support creators by paying an ongoing monthly subscription fee and, in return, receiving exclusive content or early access to new releases by authors.

How much money do science fiction authors make?

Science fiction writers can earn various sums depending on factors like their level of success, their publisher, the specific project they are working on, and the royalty rate.

According to a survey by the Authors Guild, professional writers (including science fiction authors) typically make between $20,000 and $30,000 annually on average; however, top-selling science fiction authors may generate millions per year in sales revenue.

It's important to keep in mind that most writers do not depend exclusively on writing for income; most may supplement it with other jobs or revenue sources.

How much a science fiction author makes depends largely on their ability to promote their work and build an audience, leading to more book sales and other monetisation opportunities.

How does self-publishing impact the earnings of science fiction writers?

Self-publishing can have a dramatic impact on the earnings of science fiction authors. By choosing self-publishing, authors gain more control over the publishing process and can earn a larger portion of their book's profits than with traditional publishing.

Self-publishing allows authors to earn up to 70% of their book's sale price compared to the 10-15% they might make with traditional publishing due to platforms like Kindle Direct Publishing and Barnes & Noble Press not having overhead costs such as printing, distribution, marketing expenses, etc.

Self-publishing offers authors more earnings potential as well as faster book publication times and increased reader reach. They can set their own pricing and marketing strategies while keeping full control over their intellectual property.

***

Are there any specific markets or genres within science fiction that tend to be more profitable?

There are certain markets and genres within science fiction that tend to be more profitable than others, such as these sub-genres:

Space opera: This sub-genre typically offers epic and adventure-filled tales set in outer space and is beloved among readers who enjoy fast-paced action with vibrant characters.

Cyberpunk: Cyberpunk literature often explores technological and dystopian societies, drawing in readers who enjoy gritty yet futuristic tales.

Military science fiction: This sub-genre often explores military themes and tactics set against a science fiction backdrop, making it particularly enjoyable to readers who enjoy action-packed stories with an emphasis on strategy and combat.

Post-apocalyptic fiction: This sub-genre explores what happens to humanity following a devastating event such as nuclear warfare or a pandemic and is popular with readers who enjoy survival stories that examine the human condition under extreme conditions.

Steampunk: This sub-genre often combines elements of science fiction and historical fiction and is especially appealing to readers who appreciate imaginative stories with a retro-futuristic setting.

Notably, however, the profitability of any genre or sub-genre varies based on a range of factors, including market trends, reader preferences, and the specific book or author being considered for publication.

If you want help with how to get started from scratch, we recommend you take a look at our workbook: **"How To Write A Winning Fiction Book Outline - Sci-Fi Workbook,"** which takes you from idea to publication.

3

Quick Tips For Science Fiction Writers Starting Out

We get asked the question, *"where should I start as a science fiction writer,"* a lot. So, to help you get started, here are some quick tips that might come in handy:

Read a lot of science fiction books: This will not only give you a better understanding of the genre, but also help you figure out what works and what doesn't in a science fiction story.

Take notes: As you read, make a note of what you like and don't like about the books you're reading. This will help you develop your own writing style and avoid common pitfalls.

Branch out: Don't just read books in your favourite sub-genre of science fiction. Try reading books that take place in different worlds, with different magic/political/social systems, and featuring different types of characters.

Analyse structure: Pay attention to how the author structures their story, how they reveal information, and how they build tension. This will help you develop your own writing skills.

Create a believable and immersive world: A well-crafted science fiction world can make all the difference in capturing your readers' imaginations. Think about the geography, history, culture, and magic system of your world, and make sure it all fits together seamlessly.

Research: Take the time to research different aspects of your world, whether it's geography, history, culture, or magic. This will help you create a more realistic and immersive world. Take a look at science fiction book reviews, look at the 1 and 5 stars, and compare.

Consistency is key: Make sure that everything in your world fits together seamlessly. Avoid contradictions and plot holes.

Show, don't tell: Don't just dump information on your readers about your world. Show them through your characters' actions and experiences.

Develop memorable and relatable characters: Your readers will likely be invested in your story because of the characters you create. Make them unique and relatable, with motivations and personalities that drive the plot forward.

Give them flaws: No one is perfect, and neither should your characters be. Give them flaws that make them more human and relatable.

Here are a few examples of flaws you could give to your characters:

Pride: An overly proud character can create conflict and tension in any story they appear in.

Greed: Characters driven solely by greed can make them less sympathetic in the eyes of readers.

Fear: Characters who struggle with fear can make them relatable to readers.

Anger: Characters who display anger issues can add a level of complexity and unpredictability that enhances the storyline.

Indecisiveness: Characters who find it difficult to make decisions can add tension and uncertainty to any storyline.

Insecurity: Characters who struggle with insecurity can make their story more relatable and human for readers.

Naivety: Being overly trusting of others can leave them open to potential danger in a story and could create opportunities for conflict in its pages.

Impulsivity: Characters who act impulsively often cause chaos and tension in their stories.

Motivations for your characters

Motivations are an integral component of character development. When creating characters, make sure they have clear motivations that drive their actions and decisions throughout the story. By giving your characters clear, believable motivations that resonate with readers, you can create more compelling and captivating characters who keep readers invested in your tale.

Here are a few motivations you could give your characters:

Revenge: Characters that wish for revenge against their former wrongdoer may drive their actions and decisions throughout the story, motivating every action and decision they make.

Love: Characters driven by passion can create powerful emotional stakes in their stories.

Power: Any character seeking power and influence can create tension among other characters.

Fear: Being driven by fear of inaction may spur someone to take bold steps and make difficult decisions.

Ambition: Individuals driven by ambition can take risks and make bold choices when motivated by this trait.

Survival: Characters who seek survival can add urgency and suspense to a storyline.

Justice: Characters who seek or fight for justice can create an engaging narrative thread within their tale.

4

Popular Science Fiction Novels

Science fiction is one of the most popular genres. Here are just a few of its most famous examples:

"Dune" by Frank Herbert - Set in a futuristic universe where powerful noble houses vie for control of Arrakis, an oasis planet which supplies spice melange, the novel features an intricate plot with themes encompassing politics, religion, ecology and ecological issues - making it one of the genre's classic works and frequently adapted into film or TV adaptations.

"Ender's Game" by Orson Scott Card - Set in a future where humanity is at war with an alien race known as the "Buggers," this novel follows Ender Wiggin from military school training as he becomes a commander that will lead humanity to victory against them. Exploring leadership, ethics, and the psychological toll of war, winning multiple awards along the way and being made into film and video game adaptations.

"The Hunger Games" by Suzanne Collins - Suzanne Collins' dystopian novel "The Hunger Games" takes place in a future dystopia where an oppressive government requires children from each district to compete in an annual death match known as The Hunger Games while following Katniss Everdeen from District 12, who volunteers to enter to protect her younger sister. It explores themes of power, oppression, and revolution; becoming widely successful after being made into a popular film franchise.

"The War of the Worlds" by H. G. Wells - This novel is one of the earliest examples of science fiction. It details a Martian invasion while exploring themes of colonialism, evolution, and science's limits. Since its publication, numerous adaptations of "The War of the Worlds" have been created as films, TV shows, and radio dramas; this classic also inspired numerous contemporary sci-fi works to come.

"Snow Crash" by Neal Stephenson - Set in a cyberpunk future where America has been transformed into an array of corporate-controlled territories, this novel follows Hiro as he fights a virus that infiltrates virtual reality environments and attempts to stop its spread through virtual space. Exploring themes related to technology, linguistics, and reality itself, Snow Crash has received extensive critical acclaim for its compelling world-building and fast-paced action plotting.

These books have captured readers' hearts, becoming timeless classics of science fiction with their captivating stories, memorable characters, and thought-provoking themes.

5

Common Fears When Writing A Novel

Writing any type of fiction can be a minefield of different insecurities and fears.

Here are some of the most common worries writers experience:

Fear of failure: Many writers worry that their novels won't be good enough or won't be well-received by readers. To overcome this fear, it can be helpful to remember that writing is a process, and it's normal for first drafts to need a lot of revision. Focus on the joy of writing and the satisfaction of finishing a project rather than worrying about the end result. Also, by reading books like this, you have already greatly improved your chance of success!

Fear of the blank page: Starting a new writing project can be intimidating, especially when faced with a blank page or screen. To overcome this fear, try breaking the project down into smaller, manageable tasks. Set a goal of writing a certain number of words per day, or write a rough outline of the story to help guide your writing. Start with a writing prompt and see where it takes you. Don't worry about editing at this stage, just free-write!

Fear of the editing process: Writing a first draft is just the beginning of the process, and many writers worry about the revisions and editing that come next. To overcome this fear, try to approach the editing process with an open mind and a willingness to make changes. Remember that editing is an opportunity to improve the story and make it the best it can be.

Fear of rejection: Once the novel is complete, writers may worry about submitting it to agents or publishers and facing rejection. To overcome this fear, try to remember that rejection is a normal part of the writing process. Don't take rejections personally; use them as an opportunity to learn and improve your writing.

Fear of exposure: Writing a novel can feel very personal, and some writers may worry about exposing their innermost thoughts and feelings to readers. To overcome this fear, remember that writing is a form of self-expression and that sharing your thoughts and feelings can be a powerful way to connect with readers. Share your work with trusted friends or family members first, and gradually build up your confidence in sharing it with a wider audience.

Fear of success: While it may seem counterintuitive, some writers worry about what will happen if their novel is successful. To overcome this fear, try to focus on the present moment and the joy of writing. Don't worry too much about the future, and remember that success is a journey, not a destination. Enjoy the process of writing, and let the future take care of itself.

6

Fears About Writing A Science Fiction Novel

If you're thinking about writing a science fiction story, it's normal to have some fears and worries about it.

Here are some common fears people have about writing science fiction and why you shouldn't let them stop you from pursuing your dream:

"What if my story is not original enough?"

Many science fiction stories indeed share similar themes and tropes, but that doesn't mean your story won't be unique. Your characters, setting, and plot will all be your own, and your voice as a writer will make your story distinct.

Some ideas for you:

Think outside the box: Challenge yourself to come up with ideas that are not commonly seen in science fiction stories. Look to other genres or real-life events for inspiration.

For example:

Mixing genres: Combine science fiction with another genre such as horror, romance, or mystery to create unique narratives; for instance, a sci-fi horror tale set on a spaceship could make for an interesting combination.

Alternative history: To create an alternative history narrative, imagine what might have happened if a key event had unfolded differently - for instance, what might have happened if World War II had ended differently and the Nazis established their totalitarian regime around Earth instead?

Exploring current issues: Use science fiction to explore current social or political issues like climate change, inequality, or technology, for instance, by writing stories about futures where robots have taken the place of all human workers.

Non-human protagonists: Create a story featuring non-human protagonists such as an alien or sentient robot as your main characters, for instance, one about an AI that gains self-awareness but must navigate its surroundings among humans.

Set your story in unusual settings: Take your story in an unexpected direction by setting it in an unlikely place or time that's uncommonly seen in science fiction, for example, a post-apocalyptic world where humans have devolved back to medieval-level technology.

Think outside the box! By thinking creatively and taking risks to come up with truly groundbreaking ideas, you can craft stories that stand out from traditional science fiction tropes. Use your imagination and be willing to experiment to come up with innovative and exciting plot lines!

Use your personal experiences: Draw from your own experiences or emotions to infuse your story with authenticity and uniqueness.

Here are some strategies for using personal experiences in science fiction writing:

Personal struggles: Use your experiences of grief, addiction, and mental health issues to create memorable characters with relatable and complex narratives.

Draw from travel experiences: Use your experiences travelling abroad to help create rich and original settings for your story. For example, if you have visited an exotic jungle location, that experience could serve as the basis for an entire alien planet with lush vegetation.

Experience: If your background lies within science, technology, or another discipline relevant to science fiction writing, use your expertise to craft realistic worlds and technologies for science fiction storytelling.

Relationships: Use your experience of both positive and negative relationships to develop realistic and engaging character dynamics.

Cultural experiences: Draw upon your personal experiences with different cultures to craft dynamic and inclusive worlds in your science fiction story.

Using personal experiences can add depth and authenticity to your science fiction writing by tapping into your emotions, experiences, and expertise to develop compelling tales that reflect both you and the readership alike.

Experiment with different writing styles: Try writing in a different style or tone than what you're used to. This can help you explore new ideas and find your voice as a writer.

For example:

Stream of consciousness: To create an immersive or surreal atmosphere in your story, try writing in a stream-of-consciousness style in which characters express their thoughts and emotions in an uninterrupted stream of language. This style can help give off a dreamlike or surreal vibe.

Second-person narrative: By writing your story using second-person pronouns like "you," this style creates an immersive experience for readers and makes them feel part of the action.

Multiple perspectives: Create your story from multiple points of view to provide readers with an expanded and more intricate view of its events and themes.

Experiment with non-linear narrative: Experiment with non-linear stories that present events out of chronological order to create an atmosphere of mystery and keep readers engaged as they try to piece together your tale. This technique may keep readers guessing while keeping their attention focused on your tale.

Experimenting with different writing styles and techniques is an invaluable way to find your voice as a writer and create stories that stand out. Don't be afraid to try new approaches and experiment to see which one suits your story best.

Collaborate with others: Collaborate with other writers or artists to bring new perspectives and ideas to your story.

Embrace the familiar: Don't be afraid to use familiar science fiction tropes or themes, but put your own spin on them. Focus on creating compelling characters and unique settings that readers will connect with.

Here are a few examples of including familiar elements in science fiction writing:

Make use of common sci-fi tropes such as time travel or space exploration with an original twist - for instance,
in **"Interstellar,"** characters use a wormhole to travel between space and time but must contend with relativity and time dilation during their trip.

Make use of an established theme, like artificial intelligence or alien invasion, but approach it from an unconventional viewpoint. For instance, in **"The Three-Body Problem,"** aliens do not appear as invaders but as potential solutions to Earth's issues.

Use classic sci-fi concepts such as cloning or genetic modification, but focus on their ethical and moral ramifications. For example, in **"Gattaca,"** one must navigate an environment in which genetic engineering determines one's status and opportunities in life.

By drawing inspiration from what readers know and adding your own special twist, you can craft an engaging narrative that resonates with readers while remaining fresh and exciting.

"What if I don't know enough about world-building?"

World-building can seem daunting, but you don't need to be an expert to write a compelling science fiction story. Start with a basic outline of your world and add details as you go along. You can always do research or seek feedback from others to help fill in any gaps.

"What if my characters aren't interesting enough?"

Characters are a key part of any story, but they don't have to be perfect or larger-than-life. Flawed and relatable characters can be just as compelling, if not more so. Focus on creating characters with distinct personalities and motivations that drive the plot forward.

Some ideas for you:

Give them a unique backstory: Develop a detailed backstory for each character, including their upbringing, experiences, and personality traits. This will help readers understand their motivations and actions throughout the story.

For example:

- The character grew up in a small village plagued by a supernatural curse.

Give them flaws: No character is perfect, so give your characters flaws that make them relatable and human. This can include things like insecurities, bad habits, or moral ambiguities.

For example:

- *The character has a deep-seated fear of failure that drives them to take unnecessary risks and make impulsive decisions.*

Show, don't tell: Instead of telling readers about your characters' personalities, show their traits through their actions and dialogue. This can help readers connect with them on a deeper level.

For example:

Telling: John was angry that he missed the bus.

<u>Showing:</u> John's face turned red and he clenched his fists as he watched the bus drive away. *"Why does this always happen to me?"* he muttered under his breath.

Create relationships: Develop relationships between your characters that are dynamic and complex. This can include romantic relationships, friendships, or even rivalries.

Use character questionnaires: Use character questionnaires to flesh out your characters' personalities, motivations, and backgrounds. This can help you create a more well-rounded and believable character.

Ideas for you:

- What is your character's name, age, and physical appearance?
- What is your character's occupation or role in the story?
- What is your character's backstory and how has it shaped them?
- What are your character's strengths and weaknesses?
- What are your character's goals and motivations?
- What are your character's fears and insecurities?
- What is your character's relationship with other characters in the story?
- What are your character's hobbies or interests outside of the main plot?
- What is your character's personality type (e.g. introverted, extroverted, etc.)?
- How does your character change or grow throughout the story?

"What if my story is too long or too short?"

The length of your story will depend on the complexity of your plot and the depth of your world-building. Don't worry too much about length in the early stages of writing. Focus on telling the story you want to tell, and worry about trimming or expanding it later during the editing process.

Some ideas for you:

Use a three-act structure: A three-act structure can help you organise your story and ensure that it has a clear beginning, middle, and end. This can help you avoid unnecessary tangents or plot holes.

Set a word count goal: Set a word count goal for your story based on your genre and the complexity of your plot. This can give you a benchmark to work towards and help you avoid overwriting or underwriting.

Outline your story: Use an outline to map out the major plot points and beats of your story. This can help you see where you may need to expand or trim certain scenes or chapters.

Seek feedback: Share your story with beta readers or writing groups to get feedback on pacing and length. Ask them if any parts of the story feel rushed or dragged out, and use their feedback to adjust your pacing.

Cut unnecessary scenes: During the editing process, review your story for scenes or chapters that don't advance the plot or develop the characters. Cut these scenes to tighten your story and improve its pacing. *'Cut the fluff!'* as they say.

"What if no one likes my story?"

It's natural to want others to enjoy your writing, but not everyone will. Remember that writing is a form of self-expression, and it's okay if not everyone connects with your work. Focus on writing the story you want to tell, and enjoy the process of creating something new.

Some ideas for you:

Read reviews of bestselling science fiction: Reading reviews of popular science fiction novels can give you insight into what readers enjoy and what to avoid. Use this knowledge to improve your own writing and avoid common pitfalls.

Develop a thick skin: Accept that not everyone will love your work, and that's okay. Don't take negative feedback personally, but use it as an opportunity to grow and improve as a writer.

Celebrate your successes: Don't forget to celebrate your successes, no matter how small they may seem. Finishing a draft, receiving positive feedback, or even just making progress on your writing goals are all accomplishments to be proud of.

Remember, writing a science fiction story should be a fun and creative process. Don't let your fears hold you back from exploring new worlds and characters, and don't be afraid to take risks and try new things.

Some fears specifically related to science fiction

Fear of the unknown: Science fiction often requires creating unfamiliar worlds, technologies, and societies - this can be daunting for writers unfamiliar with its genre.

Try this:

Start small: When creating your world or society, start small and build upon one aspect at a time. If you are creating an entirely new planet, for example, develop its geography and climate before moving on to its inhabitants/culture.

Use metaphors: Sometimes using familiar elements and metaphors can help readers grasp unfamiliar concepts more easily. For instance, using "bird-like" to describe an alien race gives readers visual cues that help them imagine it more readily.

Fear of being too technical: Science fiction often employs complex scientific terminology that some writers worry will be too technical for readers to grasp.

Try this:

Use familiar terms: Whenever possible, try to employ scientific terms that readers already have an understanding of. For instance, instead of "hyperspace displacement," use more accessible terminology like "jump drive" or "warp speed."

Explain the terminology: If your scientific topic requires complex terms, be sure to provide an easy-to-understand explanation in layman's terms of what each one means so your readers don't become intimidated by technical jargon. This will allow them to fully grasp your concept without feeling confused by technical terms.

Use analogies: Analogies can be an excellent way of conveying complicated ideas. For instance, using analogies could help explain time dilation likening it to a rubber band stretching and contracting as an illustration of its meaning.

Show, don't tell: Whenever possible, endeavour to show scientific concepts through actions rather than words; for instance, rather than explaining how a spaceship's engine works, show its maintenance being conducted by characters on screen.

Make sure you conduct sufficient research: Make sure that the scientific concepts you're incorporating in your story are understood thoroughly; if unsure of anything, conduct a more extensive investigation or consult experts in the field.

Fear of being too derivative: With science fiction's long history and well-known tropes, writers may fear that their work may appear derivative or unoriginal.

Fear of being taken seriously: Science fiction writers may worry that their work won't be taken seriously by literary circles and that they won't receive any credit for its creation.

Science fiction often demands extensive research and knowledge in fields like physics, biology and engineering - this can be daunting for writers without previous experience in these areas.

Fear of not being creative enough: Writing science fiction requires creativity and imagination in abundance, which may leave some writers concerned they lack what it takes to come up with truly unique and captivating ideas.

Fear of not balancing science and storytelling: Science fiction writers may fear they won't be able to strike an appropriate balance between scientific accuracy and engaging storytelling, which often poses as one of the key elements in writing science fiction.

Fear of criticism: Writing can be an emotionally charged endeavour, so some writers may fear their work being judged or rejected by readers, reviewers, or publishers.

Fear of not making an impact: Some writers may worry that their efforts won't have any lasting influence in either their genre or society as a whole and that their efforts will ultimately go unrecognised.

Try this:

Write for yourself: Although it can be tempting to want your writing to have an impactful legacy, your ultimate aim should be expressing the story you wish to tell and expressing unique ideas and perspectives through words on paper.

Focus on the journey, not the destination: Don't become too focused on making an ever-lasting impact with each story you write; rather, enjoy and develop your craft as you go forward on this writing journey. Every story written marks another step on that path to becoming an author.

Connect with readers: While you cannot dictate how your work will be received by readers, you can still connect with them and build an audience of fans. Engage with them through social media, attend conventions and events, build relationships with other writers and fans and develop meaningful relationships between themselves.

7

Science Fiction Writing Mistakes To Avoid

Novel writing can be extremely rewarding for an author, especially when they receive an excellent review. But it is all too easy to fall into the trap of bad habits in novel writing.

Here are the most common mistakes writers make and how to avoid them:

Info-dumping: Avoid dumping too much information about your world or characters at once. This can overwhelm the reader and slow down the pacing of your story. Instead, reveal information gradually throughout the story and only include what's necessary to advance the plot.

Try this:

Start in the middle of the action: Start your story in the middle of the action rather than with an elaborate introduction, to capture the reader's attention quickly while providing you with an opportunity to reveal information slowly as the narrative unfolds. This approach also offers you more freedom when revealing important pieces of information gradually throughout the narrative.

Example:

As soon as they emerged from hyperspace, alarms sounded throughout the cockpit. Captain Maria Gomez felt her heart racing as she searched the console to identify its source.

"What the hell is going on?" Jake demanded as alarms continued to sound off.

"I don't know, but we seem to be being drawn closer," Maria replied as she desperately attempted to gain control of the ship again.

Show, don't tell: Rather than telling your reader about your world or characters, show them through actions and dialogue to build stronger bonds between yourself and readers as well as a more organic understanding of world events.

Example:

Instead of simply telling readers that Aiden was a brilliant scientist, the story showed them his innovative new technology that would transform human history. Aiden sat hunched over his workbench fiddling with wires and circuits when suddenly there was a breakthrough!

"Wait," he murmured to himself as his eyes widen as he scrawled notes on his pad of paper. "What if I switched around the polarity...?"

Aiden worked tirelessly for hours, rarely stopping to eat or rest.

Focus on what's relevant: Only include details that add substance and depth to the plot and characters in your story, rather than unnecessary details that don't contribute anything new or bring any value.

Use dialogue and internal thoughts: Dialogue and internal thoughts can help reveal information about your world and characters, helping break up the exposition and make it feel more natural.

Use flashbacks and memories: Flashbacks and memories can help reveal information about your characters and world without slowing the pace of the story. They provide a seamless way of providing backstory or world-building details more organically.

Overused tropes: While familiar tropes and themes can be comforting to readers, overusing them can make your story feel clichéd and unoriginal. To avoid this, put your own spin on common tropes or create new ones altogether.

Some examples:

- **The chosen one:** A hero who is destined to save the world and possesses unique powers or abilities.
- **The evil empire:** A powerful and oppressive empire or ruler that the protagonist must overthrow.
- **The mentor:** A wise and experienced character who guides the protagonist on their journey.
- **The magical artefact:** A magical object that the protagonist must find or protect to save the world.
- **The love triangle:** A romantic subplot in which the protagonist must choose between two love interests.

While these tropes can be effective when used sparingly or freshly and innovatively, overusing them can make a story feel unoriginal or predictable.

To avoid falling into this trap, put your own spin on these common tropes or create new ones altogether. Focus on creating unique characters, settings, and plot devices that will make your story stand out from the crowd.

Weak world-building: A poorly developed world can make your story feel flat and unengaging. To avoid this, focus on creating a well-crafted and believable world with a clear history, geography, culture, and magic system.

Try doing this:

Start with research: Gather inspiration and information from real-world cultures, history, and science to create an original yet realistic world that won't feel derivative or unrealistic.

Build a clear history and geography: Consider all aspects of the history and geography of your world, including how it was formed, which events affected its development, how its land is divided among nations, etc., to create an immersive, lifelike world that feels real and lived-in. This can help ensure an engaging experience for readers.

Build distinct cultures: Develop distinctive cultures and societies within your world, including their customs, beliefs, and social structures, to help create interesting characters and conflict scenarios. This will also allow for a wide array of characters.

Use sensory details: By including smells, sounds, and textures into the story world that readers can inhabit, you can create an immersive and vibrant world for readers to immerse themselves in. This helps bring it alive for them and adds depth and dimension that readers can connect with and find captivating.

Here are a few general ideas/examples of how to include sensory details in science fiction writing:

Smells: Add unique and memorable scents to your story world, such as the metallic scent of a spaceship or sweet floral perfumes from other worlds, so your readers can better visualise and connect with your world on an emotional level.

Sounds: Use sounds to set the scene and mood of your story, such as the engine hum of a spaceship, or to heighten suspense by creating tension with an impending threat looming closer.

Textures: Deliberately describe the textures of objects within your story world, such as rough bark or the smooth surfaces of spaceship control panels. Doing this can help readers imagine physical sensations related to this world and enhance the reading experience.

Tastes: If your story world includes unique food or beverages, make sure to describe their flavours and textures in great detail to enhance readers' sensory experiences and bring more life and dimension to their world. This can make reading your tale that much more vivid.

Visuals: While visual details don't technically fall under sensory details, adding vivid and detailed visuals to your story can help readers visualise and connect with its world and characters. Use descriptive language to paint a clear image of them so readers can hold onto a lasting memory of your tale.

Remember, by weaving memorable sensory details into your story world, readers will become immersed in your characters and worlds more easily.

One-dimensional characters: Characters that are one-dimensional and lack depth can make your story feel flat and uninteresting. To avoid this, create characters with distinct personalities, motivations, and flaws. Use character questionnaires and other writing exercises to flesh out their backgrounds and make them feel like real people.

Lack of conflict: A story without conflict can make for a boring read. To avoid this, create obstacles and challenges for your characters to overcome. Use the three-act structure to map out a clear conflict and resolution for your story.

Here is an example of creating conflict in a sci-fi novel:

In a future Earth devastated by climate change and overpopulation, astronauts are sent on an expedition to colonise a new planet. Unfortunately, upon their arrival, they discover it is already occupied by an intelligent alien race.

Conflict arises when the astronauts try to communicate with and coexist with these beings, causing an internal strife within their group, political quandaries, ethical dilemmas, and physical threats from an unfamiliar hostile environment. Ultimately, both races must find ways to coexist peacefully, while finding solutions to overcome personal hurdles or conflicts to ensure survival.

By creating conflicts and obstacles for characters to overcome, this sci-fi novel provides a clear narrative that keeps readers invested. The three-act structure can help map these conflicts out and ensure that there is an engaging beginning, middle, and end with satisfying resolutions.

Here is an example of a three-act structure for the sci-fi novel idea above:

Act 1: Establishment

Act 1 opens on Earth, where overpopulation and climate change have reached alarming proportions. Astronauts are chosen to colonise another planet to prevent the human race from becoming extinct.

The astronauts encounter various problems on their journey, from technical difficulties and resource scarcity to interpersonal conflicts within their group. Finally arriving on their destination planet, however, they find out it has already been colonised by an intelligent alien race.

Act 2: Confrontation

Conflict arises as astronauts attempt to communicate and coexist with aliens from another world, yet encounter various problems, including language barriers, cultural differences, and misunderstandings.

As they attempt to form relationships with aliens, they soon discover that the alien society views humankind as a threat and sees any attempt at interaction as potentially hostile acts against their society.

The astronauts must navigate political and ethical dilemmas as well as physical threats from hostile aliens.

Act 3: Resolution

When the aliens launch an attack against the human settlement, tensions escalate rapidly.

The astronauts must use all available skills and resources to defend themselves and negotiate peace with aliens. Through interactions with these aliens, the astronauts gain invaluable lessons about themselves and humanity as a whole.

The novel concludes with humans and aliens living together peacefully and the hope for a brighter future for both species.

This three-act structure follows a classic storytelling structure, with the establishment, confrontation, and resolution providing an engaging narrative that keeps readers invested in the story.

Poor pacing: A story that is too slow or fast-paced can be difficult for readers to engage with. To avoid this, use a combination of action, dialogue, and exposition to create a balanced pace that keeps readers engaged. Seek feedback from beta readers to help identify areas where the pacing may need adjustment.

What science fiction readers want

Here are some things that science fiction readers typically want, along with why they want them, and how to create them in your writing:

Believable and immersive worlds: Science fiction readers want to be transported to new and exciting worlds that feel real and fully developed.

To create a believable and immersive world, focus on details such as the geography, history, culture, and magic system of your world. Use sensory details to make the world come alive, such as descriptions of sights, sounds, smells, and textures. For example, J. R. R. Tolkien's Middle Earth is a fully realised world with a rich history and culture that feels believable and immersive to readers.

Compelling characters: In science fiction, readers want to connect with characters that feel real and relatable.

To create compelling characters, give them distinct personalities, motivations, and flaws. Use character questionnaires and other writing exercises to flesh out their backgrounds and make them feel like real people. For example, George R. R. Martin's **"A Song of Ice and Fire"** series features a large cast of characters with complex motivations and relationships that keep readers engaged.

Epic plots: Science fiction readers want to be swept up in epic adventures with high stakes and world-changing consequences.

To create an epic plot, use the three-act structure to map out a clear conflict and resolution for your story. Include obstacles and challenges for your characters to overcome, and raise the stakes as the story progresses. For example, J. K. Rowling's Harry Potter series features an epic plot that spans seven books and involves a young wizard's journey to defeat an evil wizard and save the wizarding world.

Escapism: Science fiction readers want to be able to escape from the stresses of everyday life and immerse themselves in a world of magic and adventure.

To create a sense of escapism in your writing, focus on creating a rich and vivid world with fantastical elements that readers can lose themselves in.

Use sensory details and immersive world-building to create a sense of atmosphere that transports readers to another world. For example, Patrick Rothfuss's **"The Name of the Wind"** features a richly imagined world with detailed magic systems and a sense of wonder that allows readers to escape from reality.

8

Science Fiction Writing Checklist

Before you start to write, it is important to have a checklist of what to consider at each stage of the process. This will ensure you stay focused and hit the right notes.

Here is a checklist for each stage of writing:

Before writing:

- Identify your target audience and genre.
- Brainstorm your story idea and create a rough outline or synopsis.
- Research your world-building elements, such as magic systems or historical inspirations.
- Develop your main characters with unique personalities, motivations, and backgrounds.
- Set writing goals and establish a writing routine that works for you.

During writing:

- Use a three-act structure to guide your plot and pacing.
- Avoid info-dumping and reveal information gradually throughout the story.
- Focus on showing, not telling, through dialogue and action.
- Write with a consistent tone and point of view.
- Use sensory details to make your world and characters feel real and immersive.
- Write every day or as frequently as possible to maintain momentum and consistency.

After writing:

- Take a break and let your story sit for a while before revising.
- Read through your story with a critical eye and look for plot holes or inconsistencies.
- Cut unnecessary scenes or characters to tighten the pacing and focus on the main plot.
- Seek feedback from beta readers or writing groups to get constructive criticism.
- Revise and edit your story until you're happy with the final product.

Some additional tips to consider throughout the writing process:

- Avoid overusing common science fiction tropes or clichés.
- Create a strong opening hook to draw readers in.
- Use conflict and obstacles to keep the story engaging and suspenseful.
- Ensure that your story has a clear resolution and a satisfying ending.
- Celebrate your writing accomplishments along the way, no matter how small they may seem.

By following this checklist, you can ensure that your science fiction writing is well-developed, engaging, and consistent from start to finish.

45

9

Plotting Or Pantsing?

When writing a novel, there are two general approaches: **plotting** and **pantsing.**

Here are full explanations of each approach and its pros and cons.

Plotting

Plotting is a method of writing where the author creates a detailed outline or plan for the story before beginning to write. This can include a chapter-by-chapter outline, character sketches, and other notes to help guide the writing process.

Pros of plotting include:

- **Better organisation:** Plotting can help writers stay organised and on track with their story, making a coherent and well-structured novel.

- **Less writer's block:** Plotting can help reduce the chances of writer's block, as writers know where the story is headed and can focus on filling in the details.
- **More efficient:** Plotting can be a more efficient method of writing, as writers have a roadmap to follow and don't need to spend as much time figuring out where the story is going.

Cons of plotting include:

- **Limited flexibility:** Plotting can limit the flexibility of the writing process, as writers may feel constrained by the outline and have less room to explore new ideas.
- **Can feel too structured:** Some writers may find plotting too structured or formulaic, leading to a less creative or imaginative result.
- **Takes more time:** Plotting can take more time and effort upfront, as writers need to create a detailed outline before beginning to write.

Pantsing

Pantsing, also known as *"writing by the seat of your pants,"* is where the author starts with a general idea or concept and then allows the story to unfold as they write.

Pros of pantsing include:

- **More creativity:** Pantsing can lead to more creativity and spontaneity in the writing process, as writers explore new ideas and take the story in unexpected directions.
- **More flexibility:** Pantsing allows for more flexibility in the writing process, as writers can change direction or try new things without feeling constrained by an outline.

- **Faster writing:** Pantsing can be a faster method of writing, as writers can focus on getting the story down on paper without worrying about details or structure.

Cons of pantsing include:

- **More writer's block:** Pantsing can lead to more writer's block, as writers may not know where the story is going or how to move forward.
- **Can lead to less structure:** Pantsing can sometimes lead to a less structured or well-organised story, as writers may not have a clear sense of the overall plot or direction of the story.
- **More editing:** Pantsing can lead to more editing and revisions later as writers may need to go back and add structure or clarity to the story.
- Ultimately, the choice between plotting and pantsing is personal, and different writers may find that one method works better for them than the other.

Some writers may even use a combination of both methods, starting with a rough outline and then allowing the story to evolve as they write. The most important thing is to find a way that works for you and helps you create the best possible novel.

Common questions about plotting and pantsing

Q. Can you combine both styles of writing?

A. Yes, it is possible to combine both plotting and pantsing techniques in your writing process.

With this approach, you can sketch out an overall plan or outline for your story, while still leaving enough flexibility for creative inspiration and alterations as you write.

Example: Create an overall plot structure and character arcs while leaving specific details open-ended so they can be explored further as necessary.

This approach allows for both structure and the freedom to pursue new ideas or directions as they arise.

Q. How do I know which is best for me?

A. Deciding between plotting or pantsing when it comes to writing is ultimately up to your personal choice and writing style.

Here are a few key considerations when making this choice:

Are you comfortable with uncertainty?: Pantsing offers great creative freedom; however, its lack of clear plans may unnerve some writers.

Do you enjoy planning and organising?: Plotting requires extensive preliminary preparation and outlining, which may seem time-consuming at first but eventually adds structure and direction.

Do you have an outline for your story?: If you know exactly where it will go, with characters, plots and settings all clear in mind, pantsing may feel less intimidating. Plotting can help create a more cohesive structure in which to work.

Are you writing short fiction or novels?: Short stories tend to lend themselves more easily to pantsing, while full-length novels require more planning to maintain coherency over an extended work.

Have you tried both approaches?: If you're still undecided about which approach best meets your needs, try both on different projects (or parts of one project), to determine what feels most natural and effective for you.

At its core, the ideal approach should enable you to be most productive and creative. Don't be intimidated to experiment with various techniques until you discover which works best for you.

Q. How do I develop a plot without it feeling forced or formulaic?

A. Plotting an engaging story that stands out can be challenging, so here are a few pointers that may help:

Starting with character: An engaging protagonist with clear motivations can often propel the plot more naturally forward. Consider their goals, fears and flaws that could create conflict within their narrative to propel it further.

Add complexity: Break away from a monotonous plot line by including subplots or additional layers to your story, as well as twists and unexpected turns to keep readers intrigued and interested.

Focus on theme: A strong theme can give your story direction and purpose. Consider what message you want to send with your tale, and how the plot can support its message.

Some examples of strong themes for you:

Exploration and discovery: Science fiction stories often focus on exploring what's unknown, from space travel to exploring human consciousness.

Technology and its impact: Science fiction often explores the repercussions of advanced technologies on society, from artificial intelligence's potential dangers to genetic engineering's advantages and drawbacks.

Science fiction offers a powerful vehicle for exploring issues of identity and humanness through stories featuring robots or clones.

Science fiction can also provide an outlet for exploring social and political issues such as authoritarianism, inequality and discrimination.

Environmentalism: Many science fiction stories tackle environmental concerns and their effect on Earth, proposing possible solutions to our most pressing global problems.

Break the rules: Don't be intimidated to experiment with unconventional plot structures and devices; push yourself out of your comfort zone by looking for fresh ways to tell your story.

Get feedback: Share your plot with other writers or readers and ask for their opinion and suggestions on how you could make it more engaging and less formulaic.

Remember, an engaging plot should feel natural and driven by characters and themes rather than forced or predictable plot points. Take your time developing characters, adding complexity, and experimenting with structures until your plot feels fresh and engaging to read.

Q. How do I avoid writer's block when pantsing, and how do I stay on track when plotting?

<u>When pantsing:</u>

Take breaks: If you feel stuck or overwhelmed while pantsing, take a step back from it all for some rest and relaxation - go on a walk, read a book, or engage in brainstorming to stimulate creativity.

Change your setting: Sometimes changing up the scenery can help get you out of a writing slump. Try writing in an unfamiliar location such as a coffee shop or park to shake things up and write effectively.

Set a timer for 10-15 minutes and simply free-write: This exercise can help overcome mental blocks and spark new ideas.

Use writing prompts: If you're having difficulty coming up with ideas, writing prompts are an ideal starting point. There are numerous resources online offering writing prompts tailored towards specific genres or themes.

When plotting:

Once you have an outline in place, use it as the roadmap for your story to keep yourself on the right path and avoid writer's block.

Break it down: If you feel overwhelmed by writing, try breaking your story up into smaller parts or chapters to help focus on each section at a time and make the writing process feel less daunting.

Use scene cards: Create scene cards by writing brief summaries of each scene on index cards or sticky notes, helping you visualise your story while keeping track of what needs to happen in each one.

(We have some resources for this in the back of our: **'How to Write a Fiction Book Outline – Sci-Fi Workbook'**)

Be adaptable: While an outline can be helpful, don't be afraid to diverge from it if the story demands it. Sometimes the best ideas arise when we allow ourselves to be flexible and open up new avenues of exploration.

Q. How do I know when to stop planning and start writing, or when to stop writing and start planning?

A. Determining when it's appropriate to switch from planning to writing can be challenging for writers. Here are a few tips:

Once you have an in-depth knowledge of your characters and the setting they occupy, as well as feeling prepared to jump into writing, it is time to switch gears and begin writing your novel.

Stop writing and plan when you find yourself stuck, uncertain where your story should go or have encountered roadblocks in writing it.

Adopt a flexible approach. If you prefer planning, be open to altering your original plans if the story leads you in another direction. For pantsers, take breaks periodically to assess where the story is taking them and ensure it aligns with their overall vision.

Follow your instincts. If it feels right to switch gears from planning to writing or vice versa, trust yourself and listen to what feels right to you.

No one knows your creative process like yourself so don't be afraid to experiment and find what works for you!

10

Point Of View In Novel Writing

Point of view, or POV, is the perspective from which a story is told.

There are several different types of POV commonly used in novel writing, each with its own benefits and challenges.

Here is a detailed but easy-to-understand guide to POV in novel writing, along with tips and the benefits of each.

First-person POV

First-person POV is when the story is told from the main character's perspective, using "I" as the pronoun.

Benefits of first-person POV include:

- **Deep emotional connection:** First-person POV allows readers to get inside the head of the main character, creating a deep emotional connection with them.

- **Intimate and personal:** First-person POV can create an intimate and personal feel to the story, as readers experience.
- **Greater control:** First-person POV can give the writer greater control over the narrative, as the reader only knows what the protagonist knows.

Tips for writing in first-person POV:

- **Stay consistent with the character's voice:** The protagonist's voice should be consistent throughout the story.
- **Avoid excessive self-reflection:** The protagonist should not spend too much time reflecting on themselves or their actions, as it can become repetitive.
- **Develop other characters:** Other characters must be developed as much as the protagonist is to create a well-rounded story.

Third-person limited POV

Third-person limited POV is when the story is told from the perspective of a single character, using "he" or "she" as the pronoun.

Benefits of third-person limited POV include:

- **Greater flexibility:** Third-person limited POV offers greater flexibility over the story and the narrative.
- **Ability to create multiple characters:** Third-person limited POV allows the writer to create multiple characters with unique perspectives and personalities.

- **Increased objectivity:** Third-person limited POV offers increased objectivity, as the writer can create distance between the reader and the protagonist.

Tips for writing in third-person limited POV:

- **Establish the main character early:** The main character should be established early to help the reader identify with them.
- **Avoid head-hopping:** You should avoid switching between different character perspectives within a scene.
- **Use vivid sensory details:** The writer should use vivid sensory details to help immerse the reader in the story.

Third-person omniscient POV

Third-person omniscient POV is when the story is told from the perspective of an all-knowing narrator, using "he" or "she" as the pronoun.

Benefits of third-person omniscient POV include:

- **Greater insight into the story:** Third-person omniscient POV allows the writer to give the reader greater insight into the story and its characters.
- **Increased flexibility:** Third-person omniscient POV offers increased flexibility, as the writer can move between characters and events as needed.
- **Ability to create suspense:** Third-person omniscient POV can create suspense, as the reader knows more than the characters.

Tips for writing in third-person omniscient POV:

- **Be careful with character knowledge:** Be mindful of what the narrator knows versus what the characters know to avoid plot holes.
- **Avoid head-hopping:** It's important to avoid head-hopping, which is when the writer switches between different character perspectives within a scene.
- **Use clear transitions:** The writer should use clear transitions when moving between different characters or events.

By understanding the different types of POV and their benefits and challenges, writers can choose the best approach for their story and create a compelling and engaging novel.

11

Coming Up With An Idea For Your Science Fiction Novel

So, you've decided that now is the time for you to write your novel. But what if the will is there, but the idea is not? What do you do if you can't think of a single idea?

Here are some tips to help you pull that masterpiece out of your head:

Take inspiration from your own life: Draw on your own experiences with mystical occurrences for inspiration.

Combine different genres: Consider blending science fiction with other genres, such as romance or historical fiction.

Take inspiration from real-life stories: Read real-life stories in the news or online and use them as inspiration for your science fiction novel.

Use writing prompts: Writing prompts can be a great way to generate ideas and spark creativity.

Explore different cultures: Explore different cultures and their traditions around science fiction and mysticism for inspiration.

Play with opposites: Consider pairing characters who are opposites in personality, background, or values.

Use music as inspiration: Listen to music that evokes a specific emotion or feeling and use it for your story.

Explore different time periods: Consider setting your story in a different time or era, such as the Victorian era or 1920s.

Use a dream journal: Keep a dream journal and use your dreams for your story.

Create a character first: Create a unique and compelling character and build the story around them.

Use setting as inspiration: Choose a unique or interesting setting, such as a small town or a remote island, and use it as inspiration for your story.

Use astrology as inspiration: Use astrology to create unique character traits.

Explore different sub-genres: Consider exploring different sub-genres of science fiction, such as science fiction romance or comedy.

Use mythology as inspiration: Draw on mythology or folklore for inspiration, such as the story of Cupid and Psyche.

Explore different age groups: Consider writing a science fiction novel that features characters from a different age group than your own.

Use different perspectives: Consider writing from the perspective of a non-human character.

Read lots of science fiction books: One great way to get ideas for your own novel is to read lots of science fiction books. This can help you get a sense of what kinds of stories are already out there, and what kinds of elements and themes are common in the genre. You can also take note of what you like and don't like about different stories, and use that to inform your own writing.

Brainstorm: Think about what kind of world you want to create, what kind of characters you want to include, and what story you want to tell. Write down as many ideas as possible, even if they seem silly or far-fetched.

Choose a focus: Once you have a lot of ideas, start to narrow them down and choose a focus for your novel. This could be a particular character, setting, or theme. Having a clear focus can help you stay on track as you write.

Create your world: If your science fiction novel is set in a different world or universe, take some time to create that world. Think about what the geography, history, and culture of that world might be like. You can draw maps, create timelines, and write histories to help you flesh out your world.

Develop your characters: Your characters are the heart of your story, so take time to develop them. Think about their personalities, motivations, and backstories. You can also draw sketches or create character sheets to help you visualise your characters.

Write an outline: Before writing your novel, write an outline to help you organise your ideas. This can include a summary of the plot, descriptions of each chapter, and notes on character development and world-building.

Don't forget: We fully recommend you invest in our accompanying workbook:

How To Write A Winning Fiction Book Outline - Sci-Fi Workbook

Start writing!: Once you have your outline, it's time to start writing! Don't worry too much about making it perfect at first; just focus on getting your ideas down on paper. You can always go back and revise later.

By using these methods, you can devise unique and interesting ideas for your science fiction novel that will captivate readers and keep them engaged from beginning to end.

How do I come up with a unique and original idea that hasn't been done before?

One of the challenges of creating a science fiction novel is developing something fresh and original, especially since so many stories have already been told in this genre.

Below are some strategies to assist:

Examine real-world science: Many science fiction stories draw their inspiration from real scientific concepts or advancements, so take note of any fascinating scientific developments or discoveries and how they could be explored within a fictional setting.

Combining existing ideas in new and interesting ways: If you want to innovate your ideas further, combine existing concepts in novel and interesting ways - combining time travel with dystopian societies can create something completely original! For example, mixing these familiar topics can give a refreshing twist to old concepts like time travel.

Consider the implications of technology: Technology is a common theme in science fiction, yet you can explore its effects in surprising and novel ways. Consider how technological innovations could influence society, relationships, or even our individual experiences of human life itself.

Draw from personal experiences or interests: Your experiences or interests may provide the basis of an original and captivating science fiction narrative. Consider what inspires you, and see if there's any way you can incorporate them into a science fiction tale.

Focus on characters and relationships: Science fiction can be an intriguing genre, but what really draws readers in are its characters and their relationships. Create memorable, distinctive characters who possess unique traits with unique interpersonal dynamics to add drama and intrigue.

Remember, coming up with original and striking ideas can be challenging, so take risks and explore unconventional thoughts without fear.

12

Some Science Fiction Writing Prompts For You

Here are some creative ideas to get your creative juices flowing:

- In a world in which humans can transfer their consciousness into robots, an uprising among robots for equal rights breaks out.
- One day, an individual discovers they possess the ability to enter and manipulate other people's dreams; but as soon as they do this, they realise their actions in dreamland have real-life repercussions.
- An astronaut on an extended space mission awakens from cryogenic sleep to discover that everyone on their team has gone missing and the ship itself has sustained severe damage that cannot be repaired.
- Time travellers travel back in time to prevent an unfortunate calamity, only to change history in ways they hadn't anticipated. In a future where people upload memories to an open network, one hacker begins manipulating memories for personal gain by manipulating others' memories through online storage services.

- After a global disaster, society develops into two factions based on genetics - those who are physically strong and those with superior cognitive ability.
- In a world where all diseases have been effectively eliminated, a new virus emerges that has the ability to infiltrate and manipulate people's minds.
- A person finds they can communicate with animals but soon learns they have their own societies and secrets which cannot be divulged by any means necessary.
- After humanity has colonised other planets, a group of colonists on a distant world find evidence of an alien civilisation. Living in an oppressive society where their thoughts and opinions are closely monitored, rebels organise to overthrow its oppressive government and try to take over.
- After a global blackout, technology no longer functions and people must rely on themselves and their abilities alone for survival. In a world where one's thoughts have an effect on reality, a group of rebels discover that what they thought they knew is all an illusion.
- After an environmental catastrophe, humanity is forced to live inside domed cities as their lives depend on protection from its toxic surroundings; but then a group of rebels discover that nature has returned and it is once again inhabitable.
- In a society in which all citizens are genetically engineered to be perfect, a group of "imperfect" people revolt against their oppressors and take control. Every morning they wake up in a different body without knowing where or who they will become next.
- Future is set in a world where robots have replaced all human labour, and an unlikely group of unemployed humans start an underground rebellion against this.
- One member discovers they possess the power of time travel but it quickly becomes clear that every time they

return in time changes the course of history in unintended ways.

- After an international pandemic, society becomes divided into two factions - those who have received vaccination and those who haven't. Both factions wage war against one another.
- After an enormous solar flare destroys all electronics on Earth, survivors must learn to survive without modern conveniences and adapt to life in a new, primitive world.

Have a go at "pantsing" a few paragraphs for each idea. If any ideas feel like they have legs then start to plot a more thorough outline and think more deeply about your characters.

Our **Science Fiction Writing Workbook** can really help with this stage.

13

Plotting And Structuring Your Novel

The three-act structure is a popular plotting technique in story-telling, dividing a narrative into three segments: the **setup**, the **confrontation**, and the **resolution**.

- **The setup** introduces the main characters, their environment, and their objectives.
- **The confrontation** brings forth challenges and obstacles that the characters must overcome.
- **The resolution** resolves conflicts and concludes the story in a gratifying manner.

Conflict

Conflict propels the story and creates tension that keeps readers hooked. In a science fiction novel, conflict can be external (e.g., a societal or physical barrier between the main characters) or internal (e.g., personal fears or doubts).

To generate conflict, consider these suggestions:

Analyse your characters: One of the best ways to create conflict is to think about your characters and what they want. What are their goals and desires? What are their fears and doubts? When you have a clear understanding of your characters, you can create conflicts that challenge them and push them out of their comfort zones.

Utilise external obstacles: External obstacles are things that are outside of your characters' control, such as societal or physical barriers. For example, if your main characters are from different social classes, that could create conflict in their relationship. Or if they live in different countries, that could make it difficult for them to be together.

Introduce internal obstacles: Internal obstacles are things that come from within your characters, such as their own personal fears or doubts. For example, if one of your main characters has been hurt in the past and is afraid of getting hurt again, that could create conflict in their relationship. Or if one of your characters is struggling with their own identity or sense of self, that could make it difficult for them to connect with others.

Generate tension: Tension is what keeps readers engaged and wanting to know what happens next. You can create tension by putting your characters in situations where they have to make difficult choices, or by having them face unexpected challenges. For example, if your characters are on a road trip together and their car breaks down in the middle of nowhere, that could create tension and conflict as they try to figure out what to do next.

Build towards a climax: The climax of your story is the moment of highest tension and conflict, and it's what keeps readers on the edge of their seats. To build up to a great climax, you can escalate the conflict gradually throughout your story, creating smaller conflicts that eventually lead to a big showdown. For example, if your characters are in a love triangle, you could have them start off with small disagreements and misunderstandings that eventually lead to a big confrontation.

Develop a timeline

After establishing your story idea and characters, create a timeline to organise the plot and track significant events.

To create a timeline:

Begin with major events: First, think about the major events in your story, such as the inciting incident (what sets the story in motion), the midpoint (when the story takes a major turn), and the climax (the highest point of tension). Write these events down on your timeline.

Fill in the gaps: Once you have the major events in place, think about what happens in between. What are the smaller events and conflicts that lead up to the major events? Write these down on your timeline in chronological order.

Incorporate character development: As you're creating your timeline, think about how your characters will change and grow over the course of the story. What are the key moments of character development? Write these down on your timeline as well.

Consider pacing: Pacing is important in any story, and your timeline can help you keep track of it. Make sure there's a good balance between slower, more introspective moments and faster-paced action scenes.

Revise as necessary: As you're working on your timeline, don't be afraid to make changes and revisions. Your story may evolve as you write, and your timeline should reflect that.

Utilise plot points: Plot points are key moments in a story that move the plot forward and keep the reader engaged. These can include inciting incidents, major conflicts, and the climax.

Balance pacing: The pacing of your novel is important. Make sure you're balancing scenes of action and conflict with slower, more emotional scenes that allow the characters to develop and the relationships/romance to deepen.

Leverage dialogue: Dialogue is a powerful tool in any novel. Use dialogue to reveal character, build tension, and deepen the relationship between your main characters.

Edit and revise: Once you've completed your first draft, take the time to edit and revise. Look for inconsistencies in the plot or character development, and make sure you're telling the story you intended to tell.

Here's an example of what your timeline might look like:

Inciting incident - The protagonist discovers something.

- **Chapters 2-4:** The protagonist sets out on a journey to learn more about the object and its effect on the world.
- **Chapters 5-7:** The protagonist meets other characters and begins to form alliances.

Midpoint - The antagonist is revealed. The stakes are raised.

- **Chapters 9-12:** The protagonist and allies face smaller conflicts and obstacles in preparation for the final battle.
- **Chapters 13-15:** Climax - the final battle takes place.

Resolution - The aftermath of the battle and the protagonist's return home.

14

Creating A Compelling Opening Scene

The opening scene of your science fiction novel is the most important one you will write. You want to grab the reader by the scruff of the neck and refuse to let go of them until the very last line of your novel.

Here are some tips on how to write a brilliant opening scene:

Start with action: A great way to grab a reader's attention is to start with action. This doesn't necessarily mean a physical action scene, but rather a scene where something is happening that creates tension or conflict.

Example:

"The engines are running smoothly, Captain," said the ship's engineer, Jake, from his console.

Captain Maya Patel nodded, her eyes surveying the vast expanse of space before them. "Good," she replied, glancing over to Jake for guidance on readings.

Suddenly, the ship jolted violently, and instantly alarms went off.

Introduce your main characters: Your opening scene is a great opportunity to introduce your main characters and give readers a sense of who they are. Make sure to give readers a reason to care about these characters and invest in their stories.

Set the tone: Your opening scene should set the tone for your entire novel. If you're writing a light-hearted science fiction romance, your opening should reflect that. If you're writing a more dramatic novel, the opening should be more serious.

Create suspense: A great way to keep readers engaged from the very beginning is to create suspense in the opening scene. This can be done by starting with a mystery or a problem that needs to be solved.

An example for you:

Commander Lee had one objective in mind when she entered the desert surface of this planet: to find and retrieve data collected by lost researchers. As she searched the bleak landscape, however, something seemed to be watching her; her heart raced as her sense of danger intensified further. She reached for her weapon as it became apparent something might threaten her safety.

Use vivid descriptions: Creating vivid descriptions of the setting, characters, and events can help draw the reader in and immerse them in your story. Make sure to use descriptive language that paints a picture in the reader's mind.

Some ideas...

Prompt: In a world where humans can transfer their consciousness into robots, a revolt among robots for equal rights erupts against humans.

Opening scene:

Peering through broken windows, Dr. Cynthia Evans watched robots marching with signs demanding equal rights - and began asking herself, "What have I done?" Suddenly realising her invention had started something of a revolution, she whispered her regretful thought again: "What have I done?"

Prompt: Time travellers travel back in time to stop a catastrophe from happening, only to alter history in ways they couldn't have anticipated.

Opening scene:

Dr. Jameson could smell the ozone as he furiously adjusted the controls of his time machine, his fingers shaking with urgency as he attempted to navigate temporal currents that would bring them back to 1984. Sweat beaded on his forehead as he laboured against the resistance of the machine as they raced through time. Suddenly, something went terribly wrong when they hit an unusually fast speed and felt an uneasiness that caused their stomachs to lurch.

Prompt: In an oppressive society, where individuals' thoughts and ideas are constantly monitored and controlled by government agents, rebels plan an insurrection to overthrow it.

Opening scene:

The air was thick and filled with sweat and fear in the underground cellar, where a group of rebels had huddled together. Their hearts were racing in anticipation of what lay ahead. They had been meeting secretly and plotting.

Listening to their leader speak in her low and urgent tone, they could taste desperation on their tongues. Through their thin walls could be heard the clinking of glasses and murmurings of conversation from above, reminding them of the life they fought hard to reclaim. Cold concrete walls and floors chilled their skin as they huddled close for warmth, their eyes darting nervously around the room. Now was the time for action, to break free.

Start in the middle: Instead of starting at the beginning of your story, try starting in the middle of the action. This can create a sense of urgency and make readers want to know how the characters got to that point.

Create emotional stakes: Your opening scene should make it clear what's at stake for your main characters emotionally. This can be a great way to create tension and keep readers invested in the story.

Use dialogue: Dialogue is a great way to reveal the character and create tension. Consider starting your novel with a conversation between your main characters that hints at the conflict to come.

Example:

"Are you sure this is the right planet?" asked Lieutenant Maria Sanchez, her voice laced with scepticism.

Captain Jack Davis sighed, his gaze fixed on the swirling blue planet below them. "The coordinates check out, Maria. We're on the right track."

"But what if we're wrong? What if there's nothing here but barren wasteland?" Maria pressed, her fingers tapping nervously on her console.

"We don't have a choice," Jack replied firmly. "Earth is dying, and this is our last chance to find a new home. We have to explore every possibility."

Maria fell silent, her thoughts racing as she stared out at the planet below them.

Keep it brief: While you want your opening scene to be compelling, you also don't want to overwhelm readers with too much information. Keep your opening scene brief and to the point, with just enough detail to draw the reader in and leave them wanting more.

76

15

Creating Characters

Robust characters are vital for any novel, particularly in a science fiction story. Your characters should be relatable, captivating, and multifaceted. Writers need to flesh out personalities, motivations, and histories to create well-rounded characters that readers can empathise with.

But how do you create captivating characters that readers won't forget?

The basics

Start by establishing basic information about your characters, such as their name, age, gender, occupation, and physical appearance.

Some ideas for you:

Name: Choose a name for your character that fits the culture and setting of your science fiction world. For example, if your story is set in a medieval-inspired world, you might choose a name like "Aldric" or "Evelynne".

Age: Consider the lifespan and culture of the world you've created when deciding on your character's age. If your world has magic or supernatural elements, you might have characters that live much longer than humans.

Gender: In a science fiction world, gender roles and expectations may be different than in the real world. Consider how your characters' gender affects their experiences and interactions with others.

Occupation: Think about the types of jobs and roles that exist in your science fiction world. Characters may be warriors, robots, royalty, or have other unique professions that fit the setting.

Physical appearance: In a science fiction world, physical appearance can be even more important than in the real world. Consider the different species and races that exist in your world and how they differ in appearance. Think about details such as skin colour, hair length, and unique features like horns, wings or AI implants.

Create backgrounds

Create a backstory for each character that explains how they got to where they are in your story. This can include family history, educational background, and career path.

Some ideas for you:

Family history: Think about your character's family history and how it has shaped them. Do they come from a long line of warriors, or are they the first in their family to pursue a scientific or engineering career? Are their parents still alive, or have they passed away?

Educational background: Consider where your character was educated and what they studied. Did they attend a prestigious science school, or were they trained by a mentor in a more informal setting? Did they struggle with their studies, or were they a natural prodigy?

Career path: Think about your character's career path and how they got to where they are in your story. Did they have to work hard to earn their place, or did they inherit their position from a family member? Have they faced any major challenges or setbacks in their career?

Personal history: Consider any personal experiences that have shaped your character. Have they suffered a major loss, such as the death of a loved one? Have they faced discrimination or prejudice because of their race or background? Have they ever struggled with addiction or mental illness?

Relationships: Think about your character's relationships with others, both past and present. Have they had any major romantic relationships? Have they had close friendships or rivalries? Do they have any siblings or close family members?

Develop personalities

Give your characters unique personalities that set them apart from one another. Consider using personality tests or character questionnaires to help you flesh out their traits.

Some ideas for you:

Ambitious and driven: A character who is highly motivated and ambitious can be a great way to create conflict and tension in your story. They may be willing to do whatever it takes to achieve their goals, even if it means sacrificing others along the way.

Empathetic and caring: A character who is empathetic and caring can be a great way to create empathy and emotional resonance with your readers. They may be driven by a desire to help others and make the world a better place.

Sarcastic and witty: A character who is sarcastic and witty can be a great way to inject humour and levity into your story. They may use their humour as a defence mechanism, or as a way to disarm others.

Mysterious and secretive: A character who is mysterious and secretive can be a great way to create intrigue and suspense in your story. They may have a hidden agenda or past that they're trying to keep hidden.

Rebellious and nonconformist: A character who is rebellious and nonconformist can be a great way to challenge the status quo and create conflict in your story. They may be driven by a desire to break free from societal norms and expectations

---

Define goals and motivations

Every character should have goals and motivations that drive their actions in the story. Consider what your characters want and why they want it.

Ideas to consider:

Revenge: Your character may have a burning desire for revenge against a specific person or group. This could stem from a past betrayal, injustice, or tragedy.

Redemption: Your character may be seeking redemption for a past mistake or misdeed. They may be driven by a desire to make up for their past actions and earn forgiveness.

Power: Your character may be motivated by a thirst for power or control. They may be willing to do whatever it takes to achieve a position of authority or influence.

Love: Your character may be driven by a deep and abiding love for another character. They may be willing to risk everything to be with their loved one or to protect them from harm.

Survival: Your character may be motivated by a simple desire to survive. They may be facing a life-or-death situation and must do whatever it takes to stay alive.

Discovery: Your character may be driven by a desire to uncover a hidden truth or to explore the unknown. They may be motivated by a sense of curiosity and a thirst for knowledge.

***

Create conflicts

To make your story interesting, create conflicts that challenge your characters and prevent them from achieving their goals. This can include external conflicts, such as a love triangle, or internal conflicts, such as overcoming personal fears or doubts.

***

Add quirks and flaws

Characters with quirks and flaws are more appealing and relatable to readers. Consider adding quirks or flaws to your characters that make them more unique.

Ideas to consider:

Fear of heights: Your character could have a fear of heights that affects their actions and decisions throughout the story. This could create tension in scenes that take place at high elevations, or force the character to find alternative routes to their destination.

Picky eater: Your character could be a picky eater, creating challenges when finding food on their journey. This could also be used to show their personality traits, such as being stubborn or resistant to change.

Perfectionism: Your character could be a perfectionist, creating tension with other more laid-back or improvisational characters. This could also create conflict within the characters as they struggle to balance their desire for perfection with the realities of the situation.

Clumsiness: Your character could be clumsy, causing moments of physical comedy or tension. This could also show vulnerability and create empathy for the character.

Impulsiveness: Your character could be impulsive, which could create moments of unpredictability and tension. This could also be used to show their passion or willingness to take risks.

Build relationships

Relationships between characters are a crucial aspect of any story. Consider how your characters interact with one another and how their relationships evolve throughout the story.

Use foils

Foils are characters with opposing natures that highlight each other's differences. Consider adding a foil character to your story to create more tension and conflict.

Make them dynamic

Dynamic characters change and evolve throughout a story. Consider how your characters grow and change as the story progresses.

Test your characters

Test your characters by placing them in difficult situations and observing their reactions. This can help you better understand their motivations and personalities.

Character building - example

Name of character: Zara is an adventurous young woman living on an alien world ruled by an oppressive empire.

Age: Zara is 25 years old but, due to the conditions on Mars, appears only 18 due to their unique atmospheric conditions.

Gender: Female

Occupation: Zara works as a skilled mechanic, maintaining and repairing spacecraft that travel to and from planet. Additionally, she secretly leads a rebellion against the empire in her free time.

Physical appearance: Zara stands out with her unique look, featuring metallic silver hair and striking green eyes that look right into you. Due to the biodiversity on her planet, her skin has developed into a deep shade of blue; additionally, she sports small pointed ears as well as having a slim build.

Zara hails from an extended line of rebels who have long opposed the Empire. Both her parents were killed when she was young, leaving her to be raised by her grandmother who instilled within her a strong sense of resistance and rebellion.

Zara received her education from her grandmother, who taught her all she knows about mechanics, engineering, and fighting against the Empire. Additionally, Zara gained insight into the history of rebellions fought by ancestors like herself as she studied her history of rebellions first-hand.

Career path: Zara was drawn into mechanics by her passion, with an aim of using it against the empire. Although there have been challenges and setbacks along her way, Zara remains determined to use her knowledge to aid the rebellion and use all available means at her disposal to aid it.

Personal history: Zara has experienced many difficulties and hardships in her life, such as grieving the loss of both parents. She has struggled with anxiety and depression but finds comfort in both work and leadership of a rebellion group.

Relationships: Zara values her relationships with fellow rebels as part of her extended family, while also having a romantic entanglement that is complicated by their roles within the rebellion and associated risks they must bear.

Zara's primary motivations and goals: Her primary objective is to overthrow the empire and restore freedom to her planet, with this effort motivated by an inherent sense of justice and her wish to honour the legacy of her ancestors.

Conflicts: Zara faces numerous external conflicts, such as attempts by the empire to capture and subdue her rebel movement. Additionally, she deals with both internal struggles such as anxiety and depression as well as her challenging romantic relationships.

Quirks and flaws: Zara has an unfortunate tendency for acting impulsively and taking risks that put herself and others at risk. Additionally, she sometimes struggles with feelings of inadequacy and impostor syndrome, even with all her impressive talents and achievements.

Relationships: Zara forms close ties with another rebel leader named Luka who serves as her confidante and advisor. Additionally, she has a complex romantic connection with another rebel named Mira whom she must balance her feelings for against her responsibilities as leader of their rebellion.

Foes: Zara has many adversaries to deal with; one such adversary is Emperor Liang Zhen who personifies everything she stands against - his ruthlessness and thirst for power stand in stark contrast with her desire for justice and helping others.

Dynamic character: Zara grows throughout the story as she confronts new challenges and gains insight into herself and her place within the rebellion. As she gains more self-assurance and assertiveness while simultaneously developing more trust for those around her, her character also evolves dynamically.

Character arcs

For engaging characters to shine in any tale, their journey must include some sort of arc and development. In science fiction, this may involve them adapting to new technologies or exploring unknown worlds that alter their beliefs and values.

What is a character arc?

A character arc describes *'the transformation or journey a character goes through within a story's plot line'*, often including an alteration in beliefs, values, or behaviour.

Why is the character arc important in science fiction?

In science fiction, characters often face challenges like adapting to new technologies, exploring uncharted worlds, or encountering strange beings, making a character arc an invaluable way to help readers comprehend how these experiences impact them and change them over time.

What are some common types of character arcs?

Common types of character arcs include positive arcs, where characters grow from their experiences; negative arcs, where characters become worse over time; and flat arcs, where characters remain relatively unchanged but help change the world around them.

How can I develop an interesting character arc?

To craft an engaging character arc, consider your protagonist's backstory, goals, and flaws before considering how their journey may change over time and connect to larger themes found throughout your story.

Should all characters have an arc?

No. While main characters should experience compelling changes throughout their story arcs, supporting characters may serve other functions in your tale, such as providing comic relief or aiding plot progression.

Can character arcs change while I'm writing my story?

Yes, character arcs may shift as you draft and revise your story. Stay open to new ideas and allow your characters to flourish naturally for your story's development.

We go in depth on how to do this in our workbook: **"How To Write A Winning Fiction Book Outline - Sci-Fi Workbook."**

Don't forget that crafting engaging character arcs can help readers connect more closely with your characters and become invested in their journeys. By investing the time and energy necessary to develop compelling arcs for all your characters, you can provide readers with an immersive reading experience.

Character connection to world:

For characters to feel real, they need intimate knowledge of their world, whether through relationships with other characters or interactions with technology and society of a futuristic setting.

Create a full character profile - Make your characters come alive!

Do this for each of your main characters:

1. What is the character's name, age, and gender?
2. What is their backstory, and what events in their past have shaped who they are today?
3. What is their personality like? Are they kind and gentle, or harsh and cruel?
4. What are their goals and motivations, and what do they hope to achieve?
5. What are their strengths and weaknesses?
6. What is their occupation or role in the story, and how do they fit into the world you've created?
7. What are their likes and dislikes, and what hobbies or interests do they have?
8. What is their relationship with their family and friends?
9. What is their biggest fear, and what might trigger it?
10. What is their greatest desire, and what lengths would they go to achieve it?
11. What is their moral code, and what lines would they never cross?
12. What is their physical appearance, and how does it reflect their personality?

13. What is their skill set, and what unique abilities or talents do they possess?
14. What is their relationship with magic, and how do they use it (if at all)?
15. What is their social status or class, and how does it affect their interactions with others?
16. What is their romantic history, and what kind of partner are they looking for (if any)?
17. What is their relationship with religion, and what beliefs do they hold?
18. What is their opinion of the other characters in the story?
19. What is their greatest regret, and how does it affect their actions?
20. What are their prejudices or biases, and how do they overcome them (if at all)?
21. What is their sense of humour, and what kind of jokes do they find funny?
22. What are their eating habits and culinary preferences?
23. What is their preferred method of conflict resolution?
24. What is their attitude towards death, and how have they dealt with it in the past?
25. What kind of legacy do they want to leave behind, and how do they want to be remembered?

By the time you have completed this for each of your characters, you will have fully-rounded, believable and engaging characters that will appear in your novel.

16

How To Incorporate Emotions Into Your Science Fiction Novel

Emotions are crucial for a successful science fiction novel.

Here are some tips and examples to help you weave emotions into your science fiction novel:

Show, don't tell: Instead of stating a character's feelings, display their emotions through actions, body language, and dialogue. For example, rather than writing, *"James was furious,"* you could depict him clenching his fists, shooting someone a fierce glare, or speaking with a harsh tone.

Use internal monologue: Internal monologue allows readers to peek into a character's thoughts and emotions. Use this technique to reveal how a character feels about a situation or another character.

Example:

As she gazed up at the towering castle walls, Sophie couldn't help but feel a twinge of fear in her chest. What if she wasn't strong enough to complete her mission? What if she failed and let down her comrades?

Build tension: Create tension between central characters by introducing conflict and barriers that prevent them from uniting. This tension can evoke a sense of yearning and desire that keeps readers hooked.

Employ sensory details: Use sensory descriptions to paint a vivid picture of the setting and ambience. This can help readers feel immersed in the story alongside the characters, enhancing the emotional impact.

Example:

Sight: The sun had just begun to set, casting long shadows across the forest floor. The leaves on the trees were a riot of colours - bright reds, oranges, and yellows - signalling the arrival of autumn. As the character walked deeper into the woods, they could see shafts of light filtering through the branches, illuminating the path ahead.

Sound: The character listened as the wind whistled through the trees, rustling the leaves and causing them to dance and sway. In the distance, they could hear the sound of rushing water - the nearby river, perhaps. Closer to them, they could hear the rustling of small animals in the underbrush, scurrying away at the sound of their footsteps.

Smell: The air was thick with the scent of pine and earth - the unmistakable smell of the forest. As the character walked, they could also smell the faint hint of wood smoke in the air, perhaps from a nearby village or campsite. The scent of wildflowers and herbs also drifted on the breeze, adding a touch of sweetness to the air.

Touch: The character reached out to touch the rough bark of a nearby tree, feeling the ridges and furrows under their fingertips. They also brushed their hand against a low-hanging branch, feeling the soft, velvety texture of the leaves. As they walked, they felt the uneven ground beneath their feet, the occasional rock or root jutting up to trip them.

Taste: As the character paused to catch their breath, they pulled out a water flask and took a sip. The cool, refreshing water tasted of minerals and earth, reminding them of the source from which it came. They also reached into their pack and pulled out a small piece of hardtack, the taste of dried bread and salt filling their mouth.

Vary emotions: Don't rely on just one or two emotions throughout the novel. Vary the emotions to keep readers engaged and create a more complex and realistic portrayal of the characters.

Use dialogue: Dialogue can be a powerful tool for showing emotions. Consider how the characters speak to one another and how their words reflect their emotions.

Create vulnerability: Vulnerability is a key aspect. By showing vulnerability, you allow readers to connect with the characters on a deeper level and become invested in their story.

Employ subtext: Subtext is the hidden meaning behind what a character says or does. Use this technique to show the characters' true emotions and motivations.

Example:

Imagine a scene where Anna confesses her feelings to her love interest, Mark.

Here are some ways to infuse emotions:

- Show Anna's anxiety by having her fiddle with her hands or tap her foot.

- Use internal monologue to reveal Anna's thoughts, such as *"I can't believe I'm doing this. What if he doesn't feel the same way?"*
- Use dialogue to demonstrate Mark's astonishment or bewilderment, such as "I had no idea you felt this way, Anna."
- Incorporate sensory details to create a romantic atmosphere, like flickering candles and gentle music playing in the background.
- Vary the emotions by having Anna experience nervousness, excitement, and vulnerability simultaneously.
- Utilise subtext to reveal that Anna is taking a risk by confessing her feelings and that Mark's reaction will determine the future of their relationship.

17

How To Create A Sense Of Place And Atmosphere In Your Writing

Creating a sense of place and atmosphere in your writing can help the reader really picture the scene and imagine themselves in the thick of the action.

Here are some ways to do this in your science fiction writing:

Use descriptive language: Use descriptive language to help your readers visualise the scene. For example, if your characters are at a beach, you could describe the sound of waves crashing on the shore, the feel of the sand between their toes, and the salty smell of the ocean.

An example for you:

Captain Jones had never witnessed anything quite like the alien planet he found himself and his team on. Its sky was an intense shade of purple, while its air hung heavy with sweet floral scents. Plants boasted vibrant shades of green and pink that shimmered brightly under sunlight, yet as they explored deeper into its jungle, their team could not shake a feeling that someone was watching them closely.

Consider the setting's role: Think about how the setting can play a role in the story. For example, if your characters are in a cosy café, this could be a place where they feel comfortable and are able to connect with one another.

Use details: Use specific details to create a sense of place. For example, if your characters are at a ball, you could describe the way the light catches on the chandeliers, the sound of music filling the air, and the feel of the dancers' dresses brushing against one another.

Use metaphors and imagery: Use these to create a sense of atmosphere. For example, if your characters are in a dark alleyway, you could describe the shadows as *"clutching at them like bony fingers"* or the dim lighting as *"casting a sickly yellow glow."*

Some more examples for you:

You are standing on a barren planet where the skies are perpetually red. The wind howls like hungry wolves, tears at your spacesuit, and threatens to blow you off your feet.

In the distance, you see a structure with metal frames bent and rusted like some dying beast. Upon approaching, stenches of decay fill your nostrils like ancient monsters' breath. It is evident that this place has long since lost any life that once lived there. Nothing but death and decay have followed behind it.

Metaphors and imagery are used here to create atmosphere and set the scene, including an eerie and desolate tone for this scene.

The planet is described as an inhospitable wasteland with a consistently fiery sky; wind gusts resemble a hungry pack of wolves; one structure stands alone as though dying; decay-ridden vegetation serves as evidence for ancient monsters breathing across it all contributes to an atmosphere of desolation and danger; all thanks to using metaphors and imagery that allow readers to picture every-thing clearly!

Vary the atmosphere: Vary the atmosphere to create different moods throughout the novel. For example, a sunny park might create a cheerful and romantic atmosphere, while a rainy day might create a more melancholic or introspective mood.

Use the five senses: Use the five senses to create a sense of place and atmosphere. For example, if your characters are at a carnival, you could describe the taste of cotton candy, the smell of popcorn, the sound of carnival games, the feel of the breeze, and the sight of the colourful lights.

Create contrast: Create contrast to highlight the setting and atmosphere. For example, if your characters are in a bustling city, you could contrast the noisy and chaotic streets with a quiet and serene park where they can connect in a more intimate setting.

By incorporating these techniques, you can create a vivid and engaging sense of place and atmosphere in your science fiction novel that will immerse your readers in the story.

18

Plot Twists

A plot twist refers to any unexpected turn of events which alters the outcome or direction of a storyline. A typical plot twist involves discovering previously unknown information about characters or events within their universe that was previously hidden away or concealed from view.

The impact of a plot twist on an audience can be significant. A well-executed twist can create a sense of shock, excitement, and satisfaction in the reader. It can also add depth to characters, create a shift in the story's trajectory, and generate suspense.

To create a successful plot twist, the writer needs to lay the groundwork for it throughout the story subtly. The twist should be a logical outcome of the events that have transpired, while still being unexpected. This can be achieved through foreshadowing, misdirection, and careful planning.

Here are a few ideas that might spark your imagination:

- The protagonist discovers that they are not actually the chosen one, but rather a decoy meant to distract the real chosen one from the true mission.
- The antagonist is revealed to be a long-lost relative of the protagonist, and their motivations are not as black and white as they originally seemed.
- The magical artefact that the protagonist has been searching for turns out to be a fake, and they have unknowingly been playing into the hands of the true villain.
- A beloved mentor or ally is actually working for the enemy and has been manipulating events from behind the scenes.
- The world that the protagonist thought was a fantastical realm is actually a parallel universe, and they can travel between them.

Plot twists can take many forms, but here are three common types:

- The **"unreliable narrator"** twist, where the perspective of the story is suddenly called into question, and the audience realises that what they thought was true is not. This twist can be effective in creating suspense and adding layers to a character.
- The **"red herring"** twist, where the audience is led to believe that one thing is happening or one character is responsible for something, only to discover later that they were wrong. This twist can be used to misdirect the audience and create tension.
- The **"backstory"** twist, is where the audience learns something about a character's past that changes their understanding of that character or their actions. This twist can be used to add depth and complexity to characters and their motivations.

Here are some actionable steps to create an epic plot twist in a science fiction novel:

Foreshadowing: Foreshadowing is a great way to prepare the reader for a plot twist, without giving too much away. To use foreshadowing effectively, drop subtle hints throughout the story that something unexpected might happen. For example, if your plot twist involves a character turning out to be a traitor, you could include small details that suggest they may not be trustworthy. One way to do this might be to have other characters mention that they seem to be acting strangely, or to have them exhibit behaviour that could be interpreted in different ways.

Character development: Fully developed characters are essential for creating a believable plot twist. To develop your characters, consider their motives, flaws, and desires. For example, if your plot twist involves a character betraying their friends, you might explore why they made that decision. Perhaps they were motivated by a desire for power or wealth, or maybe they had a personal vendetta against one of the other characters.

Misdirection: Misdirection is a great way to keep readers guessing, and to create a genuinely surprising plot twist. To use misdirection effectively, lead readers to believe one thing while setting up a surprise reveal later on. For example, if your plot twist involves a character being revealed as the true villain, you might initially lead readers to believe that someone else is responsible for the evil deeds that are occurring. This could involve including red herrings or false clues that point towards another character.

Subverting tropes: Tropes are common science fiction elements that readers expect to see. By subverting these tropes, you can create a plot twist that catches readers off guard. To subvert a trope, you need to be aware of what readers are expecting, and then find a way to twist it in an unexpected direction. For example, if your story involves a chosen one who is destined to save the world, you might subvert this trope by having the chosen one turn out to be a decoy meant to distract the real hero from their mission.

Emotional impact: Finally, it's important to make sure that your plot twist has an emotional impact on readers. A good plot twist should feel meaningful and significant, and it should resonate with readers long after they've finished the book. To create an emotional impact, you might consider the consequences of the plot twist. For example, if your plot twist involves a character sacrificing themselves to save others, you might explore how this impacts the other characters and the world they live in.

Misconceptions about plot twists

Plot twists are exciting elements in storytelling, but there are several misconceptions surrounding their creation.

Plot twists have to be shocking: While plot twists can certainly be shocking, they don't have to be. A good plot twist should be unexpected and surprising, but it doesn't necessarily have to be a "gotcha" moment.

Plot twists should come out of nowhere: A plot twist should be unexpected, but it shouldn't come completely out of nowhere. It's important to foreshadow the twist and lay the groundwork for it earlier in the story, even if it's in subtle ways.

All stories need a plot twist: Not every story needs a plot twist, and forcing one into a story where it doesn't fit can feel contrived. It's more important to focus on telling a compelling story with well-developed characters.

The plot twist is the most important part of the story: While a good plot twist can certainly be a memorable and impactful moment, it's not the only important part of the story. Characters, themes, and the overall story arc are all just as important.

Once the plot twist is revealed, the story is over: A plot twist should have consequences that ripple through the rest of the story. After the twist is revealed, there should still be a story left to tell, as the characters deal with the aftermath of the twist.

Three famous plot twist examples and how you can mirror this in your own writing

The Sixth Sense: While not a traditional science fiction story, The Sixth Sense is a great example of a plot twist that caught viewers off guard. Throughout the film, viewers are led to believe that the protagonist is a child psychologist helping a troubled young boy. However, at the end of the film, it's revealed that the protagonist has actually been dead the entire time, and the boy has been helping the protagonist, who is a ghost, come to terms with his own death.

Actionable step: To create a plot twist like this, consider how you can use misdirection to lead readers in one direction, before revealing the truth in a surprising way.

Harry Potter and the Half-Blood Prince: In the sixth installment of the Harry Potter series, readers are led to believe that Severus Snape is a villain, working with the evil Lord Voldemort. However, in a surprising twist, it's revealed that Snape is actually a hero, working to protect Harry all along.

Actionable step: To create a plot twist like this, consider how you can use character development to build up a character as a villain, before revealing their true motivations and loyalties.

The Empire Strikes Back: The second film in the original Star Wars trilogy is known for its shocking plot twist, in which Darth Vader reveals that he is Luke Skywalker's father. This twist was unexpected and had a profound impact on the story and the characters.

Actionable step: To create a plot twist like this, consider how you can use foreshadowing to set up the twist, while also keeping it unexpected and surprising. You might also explore how the twist will impact the characters and the story as a whole.

Common questions about plot twists

Q. How can I come up with an effective plot twist?

A. A good plot twist should be surprising while still making sense within the context of the story. Consider what readers expect will happen and subvert those expectations while still satisfying readers. You could draw inspiration from real events or other stories for surprising and unique plot twists.

Q. When is the optimal time to introduce a plot twist?

A. Timing for any story or plot twist depends on both its context and pacing, keeping readers engaged and adding excitement while not disrupting its flow too early or too late. As a general guideline, introducing one when readers have invested themselves into the narrative but before reaching its climax would be ideal.

Q. How should I arrange my story's plot twists?

A. This depends on the length and complexity of your narrative. Too many twists can become too convoluted or complicated for audiences, while too few could render your tale predictable. As a general guideline, aim for one or two major plot twists which have an immediate effect on your tale.

Q. What are some examples of well-known sci-fi plot twists?

A. Some famous sci-fi plot twists include Darth Vader being revealed to be Luke Skywalker's father in **"The Empire Strikes Back,"** The planet of the apes actually being Earth, and Tyler Durden being merely imagined by its narrator in **"Fight Club."**

19

Red Herrings

Have you ever read a book that kept you guessing until the end? That is thanks to the skill of writing red herrings.

A red herring is a literary device that is used to mislead readers or viewers. Essentially, a red herring is a false clue that is intended to throw readers off track and keep them guessing.

Red herrings are used for a variety of reasons. In some cases, they may be used to build suspense and keep readers engaged. By introducing false clues, authors can create a sense of mystery and intrigue, which can make the eventual reveal all the more satisfying.

In other cases, red herrings may be used to add complexity to a story. By including false leads and misdirection, authors can create a story that is more layered and nuanced, with multiple threads that eventually come together in a satisfying way.

Finally, red herrings can be used to make a plot twist even more surprising. By leading readers down one path, and then revealing that the truth is something entirely different, authors can create a twist that catches readers off guard and leaves a lasting impression.

What's the difference between a red herring and a plot twist?

The purpose of a red herring is to create suspense and make the eventual reveal more satisfying.

On the other hand, a plot twist is a significant change or revelation that happens in the story. Plot twists are used to keep readers engaged and to add complexity to the story. Unlike a red herring, which is a false clue meant to mislead readers, a plot twist is a genuine surprise that changes the direction of the story.

To put it another way, a red herring is a deliberate attempt to deceive readers, while a plot twist is a genuine surprise that changes the direction of the story. While both devices can be effective in creating engaging stories, they serve different purposes and are used in different ways.

Red herrings in famous novels

The Lord of the Rings: In J. R. R. Tolkien's epic series, several red herrings keep readers guessing. For example, the character Boromir is set up as a villain beforehand in the story. He's ambitious and aggressive and tries to take the ring from Frodo at one point. It's revealed later that Boromir was floundering with the temptation of the ring and that he eventually sacrifices himself to cover Frodo.

Game of Thrones: In George R. R. Martin's "A Song of Ice and Fire" series, there are several red herrings that keep readers guessing about who the ultimate villain of the story will be. In the series, readers are led to believe that the Lannisters are the main villains, particularly Cersei and Jaime. As the story progresses, it becomes clear there are other forces at work and that the true villain is someone else.

Harry Potter and the Goblet of Fire: In the fourth book in J. K. Rowling's "Harry Potter" series, readers are kept guessing who's responsible for the dark events that are happening in the story. Throughout, readers are led to believe that one of the new characters introduced in the book, particularly Mad-Eye Moody or Barty Crouch Jr., is the culprit. The true villain is revealed at the end to be a completely different character.

How to create red herrings in your science fiction novel

Consider your story's central mystery or conflict: To create red herrings, you need to have a central mystery or conflict that you want to mislead readers about. This might be the true identity of the villain, the location of a magical artefact, or the outcome of a battle.

Develop false leads: Once you've identified your central mystery or conflict, start developing false leads that will mislead readers. For example, if your story is about the search for a magical artefact, you might introduce false clues or characters that seem to be leading the protagonist in the wrong direction.

Use misdirection: Misdirection is a key element of creating effective red herrings. To use misdirection effectively, you need to lead readers in one direction while setting up a surprise reveal later on. For example, you might use foreshadowing to make readers believe that a particular character is the villain, only to reveal later on that they were actually a red herring.

Keep it believable: While red herrings are meant to mislead readers, they still need to be believable within the context of your story. Make sure that your false leads are plausible and don't strain readers' suspension of disbelief.

Reveal the truth: Finally, make sure that you reveal the truth in a satisfying way. The reveal should be surprising, but it should also make sense within the context of your story.

20

Using Descriptive Language

Using descriptive language is crucial because it contributes to the creation of a vivid and fully realised world for your readers. It enables them to mentally picture the setting, characters, and events. This can make the story seriously captivating and critical.

But be careful not to use too much flowery language because it can make the reader confused and cause them to lose interest in the story. The reader may become overwhelmed and lose track of what's going on if we fill every sentence with detailed descriptions. Using too many adjectives, such as "ethereal" and "diaphanous," for instance, when describing a character might make the reader wonder what the character actually looks like.

Instead, the selective and deliberate use of descriptive language is essential. Make sure that the words you choose add meaning and depth to the story. For instance, instead of describing a character with a lot of adjectives, concentrate on one or two key details that are crucial to the story. For instance, *"Her hair was as dark as midnight, and her eyes sparkled like emeralds."*

Read the two descriptions below. The first paragraph shows how using descriptive language sparingly but effectively can world-build for the reader by offering rich and detailed language to set the scene. The second goes way too overboard with the flowery language and serves to muddy the waters, confusing the reader.

An example of subtle yet effective, descriptive language:

The enchanted forest was a place of wonder and mystery. The trees were tall and gnarled, their branches twisting and turning like serpents. Sunlight filtered through the canopy, casting dappled shadows on the forest floor.

The air was thick with the scent of pine and earth, and the sound of rustling leaves and singing birds filled the air. As I walked deeper into the forest, I could feel the magic pulsing around me, like a living thing. It was as if every tree, every stone, and every blade of grass were imbued with some ancient power.

I knew that I was in a place of great importance and that the secrets of the universe were hidden within these woods.

An example of overkill:

The enchanted forest was a place of wondrous and incomprehensible mystery. The tall and gnarled trees were imposing and formidable, their branches twisting and turning with serpentine grace. The shimmering sunlight filtered through the verdant canopy, casting an ethereal and ineffable radiance upon the forest floor. The air was thick and heavy with the heady aroma of fragrant pine and rich, fertile earth, and the mellifluous sound of rustling leaves and sweetly singing birds filled the enchanted atmosphere with a symphony of dulcet melodies.

As I walked ever deeper into the labyrinthine heart of the forest, I could feel the immutable magic pulsing around me, like a throbbing, pulsating beat of a living thing. It was as if every tree, every stone, and every blade of grass were imbued with some ancient and profound power, resonating with arcane energy beyond my mortal comprehension.

Your descriptions must ensure the reader can picture the scene, but don't be tempted to show off your perceived prowess with the English language and go overboard to the point where your writing is so clogged up with fluff that the descriptions can't shine.

Well-chosen words do the job better than long, convoluted sentences.

21

Writing Dialogue In Your Science Fiction Novel

Dialogue is like the beating heart of a story - it's what gives it life and energy, and allows readers to really connect with the characters and the world they inhabit.

Without dialogue, a science fiction novel can feel flat and lifeless, with no real sense of personality or character. And let's not forget the pure joy of reading well-crafted dialogue - the snappy one-liners, the clever banter, the emotional confessions. It's like a little glimpse into the characters' lives, and it can be so satisfying to watch them interact and grow.

Dialogue allows readers to get to know the characters on a deeper level, to see what makes them tick, what motivates them, and how they interact with one another. It can reveal their fears, their dreams, their quirks, and their flaws.

And let's be real, who doesn't love a good character flaw?

But dialogue isn't just about character development; it also serves a critical role in moving the plot forward. Through conversation, characters can share important information, make plans, and lay out their goals and ambitions. They can argue, scheme, and negotiate, all of which can have huge implications for the story as a whole.

How to show different emotions using dialogue

Dialogue is a powerful tool when it comes to conveying emotions in a science fiction novel! You see, words have a way of capturing the full range of human experience - from joy and excitement to fear and sorrow, and everything in between. And when those words come from the mouths of your favourite characters, well, it's like an emotional rollercoaster!

Let's start with joy and excitement.

When characters are feeling happy and pumped up, their dialogue can reflect that energy and enthusiasm.

They might use lots of exclamation points, shout out their victories, and revel in their accomplishments.

For example:

"I did it! I actually did it!" exclaimed the young mage, her face lighting up with a huge grin. "I summoned the fire demon!"

Now, on the other end of the spectrum, we have fear and sorrow.

When characters are facing danger or heartache, their dialogue can be much more subdued and tense.

They might speak in hushed tones, struggle to find the right words or break down into tears.

For example:

"I don't know if we're going to make it out of here alive," whispered the warrior, her voice trembling with fear. "There are just too many of them."

And of course, there's anger - one of the most powerful emotions of all. When characters are feeling furious, their dialogue can be down-right explosive.

They might shout, insult, or even threaten one another.

For example:

"You think you can just waltz in here and take what's mine?" roared the dragon, flames shooting from his nostrils. "Think again, little human."

But emotions aren't always so cut and dry - sometimes they're mixed and complex, like love and longing. When characters are dealing with these feelings, their dialogue can be full of nuance and subtext.

They might flirt, tease, or dance around the subject without ever quite saying what they mean.

For example:

"I know we come from different worlds, and that there are so many things standing in our way," the elven princess said, her eyes locked on the human knight. "But I can't help the way I feel."

How you can convey pace using dialogue

The way characters speak to one another can tell readers a lot about the speed and urgency of a scene. And when it's done right, it can make for one thrilling ride!

For example, when characters speak quickly and in a panicked tone, it can convey a sense of urgency and danger.

They might speak in short, clipped sentences, leaving out unnecessary words or details. This can create a sense of tension and excitement, as readers feel like they're right in the middle of the action.

For example:

"Run! They're coming!" yelled the young hero, his heart pounding in his chest. "We have to get out of here, now!"

On the other hand, when characters speak more slowly and deliberately, it can convey a sense of calm or even tension.

They might take their time, carefully choosing their words or pausing for effect. This can create a sense of anticipation, as readers wait for the next shoe to drop.

For example:

"I have something to tell you," the wizard said, his voice low and measured. "Something that might change everything."

And let's not forget about silence. Sometimes, the absence of dialogue can be just as powerful as the words themselves.

A scene with no dialogue at all can create a sense of stillness or calm, while a scene with lots of interruptions or overlapping speech can convey a sense of chaos or conflict.

For example:

The battle raged on, with swords clashing and magic crackling through the air. The heroes fought with all their might, but it seemed like the enemy was endless. They spoke not a word, each lost in their own thoughts and fears.

So you see, dialogue in a science fiction novel can do so much more than just convey information - it can also convey a sense of pace and urgency, bringing the story to life in a way that's thrilling and engaging.

Some common questions about dialogue

Here are some frequently asked questions and their responses about writing dialogue for your science fiction novel:

Q. How do I write realistic dialogue for my science fiction characters?

A. To write realistic dialogue, first think about how your character(s) would likely speak, taking into account their background, personality, and the environment they exist in. Pay special attention to their word choice, grammar, and syntax, as this will give your dialogue a realistic touch. Listening to real people speak may provide additional inspiration as well.

Q. How can I ensure each character has an identifiable voice?

A. Each character should possess a distinct tone that reflects their personal and cultural backgrounds when crafting dialogue for them. Read their lines out loud before writing their dialogue lines to be certain that their dialogue stands out from that of other characters.

Q. How much dialogue should be written?

A. While there's no hard and fast rule regarding how much dialogue should be written, it is important to strike a balance between description, action, and dialogue to keep your story moving along and keep readers interested in reading your tale. Aim for a combination of dialogue, narration and action for maximum reader engagement and to keep their attention.

Q. How can I avoid stilted or forced dialogue?

A. Dialogue that sounds stilted or forced can occur when its language is overt or doesn't sound natural, such as when characters express their thoughts directly through speech rather than through subtext, body language, and actions. Read your dialogue out loud to test its naturalness before making changes as needed.

Q. Should I use sci-fi jargon in my dialogue?

A. Using sci-fi jargon can add authenticity to your story, but be careful that its usage doesn't compromise clarity. Make sure the reader can comprehend what's being said through context; too much jargon could become confusing or overwhelming to the reader.

22

How To End Your Novel

Good endings are absolutely crucial when it comes to writing a successful science fiction novel. And if we're being honest with ourselves, the ending is usually the scene we cannot get out of our heads before we even start writing. It rattles around in the brain, and you cannot stop thinking about how cool it would be if 'xyz…' happened. The content of the novel is just all the scenes that lead up to this epic, blockbuster ending.

The ending is the last thing your readers will experience, and it's what will stay with them long after they've finished the book. If your ending isn't up to scratch, it can leave a bad taste in their mouth and prevent them from recommending your book to others.

A good ending is essential because it provides closure for the reader and resolves any questions or conflicts from the story. It's the ultimate payoff for everything that's come before, and it can leave readers feeling satisfied, moved, or even changed.

A strong ending can also help solidify your reputation as a writer, building your brand and attracting new readers to your work.

But what happens if your ending isn't good?

Unfortunately, it can have some serious consequences for your writing business. Readers may leave negative reviews or give up on your work altogether, hurting your sales and damaging your reputation. You may also struggle to get your work published in the future, as editors and agents will be hesitant to take on a writer with a track record of weak endings.

There are so many ways to wrap up a story, each with its own unique twists and turns. Let's explore some of the many ways you could end your science fiction novel - some of which might just surprise you!

The happy ending

This is the classic way to end a story, with all loose ends tied up and the heroes riding off into the sunset. Think **"The Lord of the Rings"** or **"Harry Potter and the Deathly Hallows."**

How to do it:

- Ensure that all loose ends are tied up, so readers feel a sense of closure.
- Give readers a satisfying payoff for the challenges the characters have faced.
- End on a note of hope and optimism, so readers feel uplifted and inspired.

The bittersweet ending

This is a more complex and nuanced way to end a story, where the heroes may have achieved their goals but at a cost. Think **"The Hunger Games"** or **"The Dark Knight Rises."**

How to do it:

- Make sure the ending feels earned and in line with the story's themes.
- Use the ending to highlight the costs and sacrifices that the characters have made.
- Give readers a sense of emotional complexity, with both joy and sadness coexisting.

The open-ended ending

This is where you leave some things unresolved, allowing readers to speculate and imagine what might happen next. Think **"Inception"** or **"The Giver."**

How to do it:

- Decide which questions to leave unanswered and which threads to tie up.
- Provide enough information for readers to draw their own conclusions.
- Make sure the ending feels intentional and not a cop-out.

The twist ending

This is where you pull the rug out from under your readers, revealing a shocking surprise at the end. Think **"The Sixth Sense"** or **"Fight Club."**

How to do it:

- Plant clues throughout the story that will lead readers to the twist, but make them subtle enough that readers won't catch on too early.
- Make sure the twist is earned and doesn't feel like a cheap trick.
- Ensure that the twist is satisfying and doesn't leave readers feeling cheated.

The tragic ending

This is where everything falls apart and the heroes are left with nothing. Think **"Romeo and Juliet"** or **"Game of Thrones"** (book version).

How to do it:

- Make sure the ending feels earned and is in line with the story's themes.
- Give readers a sense of catharsis, even if it's a painful one.
- Use the ending to make a powerful statement about the human condition.

The ambiguous ending

This is where you leave things deliberately unclear, allowing readers to draw their own conclusions. Think **"Blade Runner"** or **"No Country for Old Men."**

How to do it:

- Decide which questions to leave unanswered and which threads to tie up.
- Use the ending to encourage readers to think critically about the story's themes and messages.
- Make sure the ending feels intentional and not a cop-out.

The epilogue

This is where you show what happens to the characters after the main events of the story have concluded. Think **"The Return of the King"** or **"The Last Battle."**

How to do it:

- Use the epilogue to tie up any loose ends that couldn't be addressed in the main story.
- Give readers a sense of closure and resolution.
- Use the epilogue to hint at the characters' future without revealing too much.

The flashback ending

This is where you reveal a key piece of information that changes everything. Think **"The Usual Suspects"** or **"The Prestige."**

How to do it:

- Use the flashback to reveal something that changes the reader's understanding of the story.
- Make sure the revelation feels earned and isn't too obvious.
- Use the flashback to deepen the themes and messages of the story.

The meta ending

This is where you break the fourth wall and reveal that the story is just a story. Think **"Stranger Than Fiction"** or **"The Never-Ending Story."**

How to do it:

- Use the ending to comment on the nature of storytelling itself.
- Make sure the ending feels earned and isn't too gimmicky.
- Use the ending to make a statement about the role of stories in our lives.

The 'choose-your-own-ending' ending

This is where you give readers multiple options for how the story could end, allowing them to choose their own adventure.
Think **"Bandersnatch"** or **"The Stanley Parable."**

How to do it:

- Use the ending to give readers agency and a sense of ownership over the story.
- Make sure the different endings are distinct and meaningful.
- Use the endings to highlight different aspects of the story's themes and messages.

How to arrive at the ending you want

Ensuring that you arrive at the ending you want in your science fiction novel can be a challenging task, but with the right plotting techniques, it's definitely possible!

Here are a few tips to help you get there:

Start with the ending in mind: Before you begin writing your novel, make sure you have a clear idea of how you want it to end. This will help you plot out the story in a way that builds towards that ending.

Create a detailed outline: Once you know how your story will end, create a detailed outline that breaks down each chapter and scene. This will help you stay on track and ensure that each part of the story is leading towards the ending you want.

Use the three-act structure: Make sure that each act has a clear goal and conflict, and that each scene moves the story forward.

Use foreshadowing: By dropping hints about the ending throughout the story, you can create a sense of inevitability and make the ending feel earned.

Revise and refine: As you write, be open to making changes to your outline and story to ensure that you're heading towards the ending you want. This may mean cutting scenes that aren't working or adding new ones that build towards the ending.

Get feedback: Once you've finished your draft, get feedback from beta readers or writing groups. This can help you identify areas where the story isn't working and make changes to ensure that you're heading towards the ending you want.

With a little planning and hard work, you can create a story that builds towards a satisfying and powerful conclusion.

Some questions about endings

Q: How can I know when it's time to end my novel?
A: Your novel should be considered complete when all major plot points have been resolved and character arcs completed - creating an overall sense of closure and completion in its storyline.

Q: How should a science fiction novel typically end?
A: Some common methods to wrap up such novels include using twist endings, bittersweet or ambiguous endings or satisfying conclusions which tie up all loose ends.

Q: How can I ensure the end of my novel is satisfying?
A: A satisfying conclusion should resolve major plot points and character arcs organically and logically while leaving readers feeling like their story has reached an appropriate conclusion. It should also elicit emotional resonance while giving readers a sense of closure.

Q: Should I leave room for a sequel when ending my novel?
A: This depends entirely on your intentions for the story. If you

intend on continuing the story in another instalment, then leaving loose ends or unanswered questions open is perfectly acceptable; just ensure the conclusion of your first book remains satisfying on its own terms.

Q: How can I avoid predictable or cliche endings?

A: To prevent predictable or cliched endings from being too predictable, try subverting reader expectations by going for something unconventional and more satisfying for your story than expected in its genre. Try considering what would create the most emotionally powerful conclusion rather than what might be expected within it.

Some ideas for endings

- The hero defeats the evil villain and saves the world from destruction.
- The hero discovers a hidden power or magical artefact that helps them defeat the villain and restore peace to the land.
- The hero sacrifices themselves to save the world, but their actions inspire others to continue the fight.
- The hero realises that the true enemy was within themselves all along, and overcomes their inner demons to save the world.
- The hero and the villain team up to defeat a greater threat, but the villain ultimately sacrifices themselves for the greater good.
- The hero must make a difficult choice that determines the fate of the world, and they choose the selfless option that saves others at their own expense.

23

Science Fiction Novel Book Titles

An effective science fiction book title should give readers an indication of the story's theme or central conflict while simultaneously sparking their interest and keeping them reading the entire novel.

Memorable and distinctive title: A memorable and distinctive title can make a book stand out in an overcrowded market, helping the book to stand out and be easily remembered by its target readership. It should be unique yet straightforward.

Tone and mood: When choosing a title for a story, the title should convey its tone and mood, whether grand and majestic or dark and gritty.

The usage of common words: Some frequently encountered words found in science fiction book titles include "star," "space," "galaxy," "planet," "war," "future," "alien," and "time."

Length of title: Science fiction book titles come in all lengths and types; most tend to be concise and memorable. A lengthy title could become unwieldy and impossible to keep track of!

Tips for crafting an epic science fiction book title:

Brainstorm keywords relating to your story: Consider the themes, characters, and settings of your tale before brainstorming keywords that could make for an arresting title.

Explore various word combinations: To ensure your title stands out and is representative of your story, experiment with various word combinations until you come up with one that captures both its significance and your memories.

Consider your story's tone and mood: Take into consideration the tone and mood of your story when selecting its title, such as an epic space opera called **"Galactic War,"** while **"Dark Stars"** could work better for dystopian sci-fi stories.

Use descriptive, emotive language: When selecting words for your story, make sure they convey their theme and tone effectively.

Gain feedback: Seek feedback on your title from friends, family, and fellow writers before initiating an opinion poll to gauge reactions from your target audience.

Consider that your book title is an integral component of its marketing and can sway potential readers' decisions to read your work. By spending the extra time to craft an attention-grabbing title for science fiction novels, you increase the odds that readers will pick your book up and make it stand out in a competitive market.

Some common questions about book titles

Q. Should I include the genre in the title?

A. While including genre in your title isn't necessary, doing so can help readers quickly identify what type of book they're searching for; for instance, **"Space Odyssey"** makes it clear that it belongs to the science fiction genre.

Q. Can I change the title after publication?

A. Although changing your book title after publication is possible, doing so could cause confusion for readers who may have already purchased or reviewed your work. Therefore, it's best to select a strong title at the outset and stick to it throughout. Some platforms may not let you change your title after it is published.

Q. Should I select a catchy or descriptive title?

A. In an ideal scenario, your title should combine catchiness and specificity to accurately reflect your story while remaining memorable and distinctive.

Q. How can I check that my title is available?

A. Researching titles that already exist will help ensure there are no legal issues or confusion resulting from them, whether through online bookstore searches, Google searches, or the U.S. Patent and Trademark Office's trademark database.

Q. Can book titles be too creative?

A. While unique titles can add flair to your book, make sure they accurately represent its tone and themes. Use words that are easy for readers to comprehend, rather than something too difficult or unfamiliar that could put off potential readers.

24

Science Fiction Writing Word Count

Science fiction writing word counts may differ depending on your story's genre, the intended audience and publishing house guidelines; however, there are some general rules you should abide by when creating science fiction works.

Short stories typically comprise **1,500 to 7,500 words** and should be brief and to the point, featuring few characters and plot lines.

Novellas typically range between **20,000 and 50,000 words** in length and offer more complex plot lines and character development than short stories.

Novels typically range between **60,000 and 100,000** words or more, providing greater scope for plot lines, character development, and world-building. It's important to keep in mind that different publishers have various requirements regarding word counts when publishing manuscripts; so before submitting yours, you must do your research beforehand.

Your science fiction writing length should ultimately depend on the needs and expectations of your intended audience. Focusing on crafting the best narrative rather than being limited by word count should be your aim.

Here is a reminder of how to ensure your story stays on track:

Plan your story: Before you begin writing, take time to plan out your story. This could involve creating an outline, developing characters, and selecting key plot points. Doing this helps keep you focused and prevents you from deviating from the intended path.

Our workbook, **"How to Write a Winning Fiction Book Outline – Sci-Fi Workbook,"** will help you do this perfectly.

Focus on the main plot: Subplots can add depth to your story, but you must stay focused on the main one. Doing so helps avoid unnecessary detours and keeps your narrative moving forward.

Keep the pacing in mind: A successful science fiction novel should maintain a steady pace that keeps readers interested. Be mindful of this aspect and avoid lingering on any one scene or detail for too long.

Edit and revise: Once your first draft is complete, take time to edit and revise it. Doing this will help remove any unnecessary dithering and guarantee your story stays on track.

Remember, writing a science fiction novel is an adventure, and it's essential to focus on the story first and foremost. Word count may be important, but it should never be your sole measure of success. Keep writing; stay committed to your project, and with time, you'll develop your own distinct voice and style.

25

Science Fiction Book Cover Tips

They say you should never judge a book by its cover. Well, unfortunately, we all do this. A good book cover is one of the most important ways to attract readers, so it must encapsulate the theme and tone of the book.

To create the perfect science fiction novel book cover, consider the following advice:

Research other science fiction book covers: When selecting a genre book cover that interests you, explore other covers in that genre and pay close attention to details such as colour schemes, typography, and imagery.

Consider hiring a professional book cover designer: Consider engaging the services of a science fiction book cover designer to craft a cover that accurately represents your book while drawing in potential readers. They will work closely with you to produce something that catches the eye and draws readers in.

Discuss your vision for the cover: Provide your designer with clear guidelines as to the themes, tones, and imagery you would like represented on your book cover design. Provide any reference images or ideas to aid the creative process.

Consider typography: Typography is an integral element of book covers. Select fonts that are legible while still reflecting the tone and theme of your book.

Make use of futuristic designs: Science fiction often incorporates futuristic technologies and designs, so incorporate those features into your cover artwork. Consider incorporating metallic colours, geometric shapes, or other design elements that reflect futuristic settings into the design of your cover.

Gather feedback: Seek input on your cover design from friends, family, and fellow writers; even running a poll on social media could help gather opinions from your target audience.

Here is an example post you could put out to ask for feedback:

Hi everyone! I'm so excited to announce that I am nearing completion of my science fiction novel and preparing to unveil its cover! Covers are so important when it comes to book marketing, so I want them to truly represent my story's theme and message.

That is where I need your assistance! I welcome any and all honest opinions and feedback on the cover design, from colours, font, imagery, and tone or theme representation to whether it fits accurately within its story universe and any potential enhancements or changes needed.

Your input would be of immense help as I finalise the cover design, so please take a look and share your opinions with me. I appreciate all feedback and am deeply appreciative that you took the time to help. Thank you again.

"Best, "[Your Name]"

Make sure it meets industry standards: Make sure that your book cover conforms with industry standards for book cover design, such as size, resolution, and file format requirements. This will ensure it is printed and displayed correctly across platforms.

Remember, your book cover is often the first impression readers will get of your novel, so it must capture its story accurately. By following these steps and working with an expert book cover designer, you can craft an outstanding science fiction book cover that attracts potential readers' eyes.

Some common things found on science fiction book covers:

Here are a few examples:

Futuristic or technological imagery: Many science fiction book covers depict futuristic or technological imagery, such as space-ships, robots, or advanced technologies.

Dystopian or post-apocalyptic imagery: Book covers featuring dystopian or post-apocalyptic science fiction usually feature images depicting abandoned cities, barren landscapes, or other symbols of an unravelled society.

Science fiction books that explore alien life or extraterrestrial exis-tence often depict bizarre creatures, otherworldly landscapes, or bizarre environments as part of their plot lines.

Bold typography: Science fiction book covers are often marked by bold and eye-catching typography, often using futuristic or unconventional fonts for title and author names.

As for colour schemes, science fiction book covers often employ dark and moody hues such as navy blue, black, and grey, as well as metallic tones like silver and gold, to create futuristic or technolog-ical looks. Bright neon shades may also be employed for an added futuristic or technological twist; ultimately, however, their use depends on the story or theme behind each book in this genre.

Some common questions about book cover design

Q. What constitutes an excellent science fiction book cover?

A. A great science fiction book cover should accurately represent its story and themes while remaining visually pleasing and eye-catching to capture readers' interest in a crowded market. It should stand out against competitors and attract potential readers' interest.

Q. Should I design my book cover myself or hire a professional?

A. Without previous graphic design experience and an eye for visual aesthetics, professional book cover designers who specialise in science fiction should usually be your go-to solution when creating book covers that accurately represent their book and attract potential readers. They will work closely with you to craft an engaging image that accurately represents it while simultaneously drawing readers in.

Q. What should I keep in mind when working with a book cover designer?

A. When working with a book cover designer, be clear about the themes, tone, and imagery you would like conveyed on your book cover. Provide any reference images or ideas you have that might aid the design process, and be open to feedback and revisions throughout the design process. It is also crucial that effective communication be maintained, as this will facilitate successful results and allow revisions to happen faster if necessary.

Q. How important is typography on my book cover?

A. Typography is an essential component of any book cover design, from science fiction to romance novels. Select fonts that are legible while complementing the tone and theme of your novel. Proper typography can make your work easily recognisable and stand out among its competitors.

Q. What are some common mistakes to avoid when designing a science fiction book cover?

A. Mistakes to avoid when designing a science fiction book cover include using overused or generic imagery, having too-busy designs, or choosing colours or typography that don't accurately portray its genre or tone.

26

Editors And Proofreaders

Editors and proofreaders are incredibly important in the 'page-to-published' process for authors. They help to develop a weak story-line, weed out boring, redundant characters, and sharpen up a dialogue throughout your novel. But firstly, how do you know which type of editor you need?

Here are different types of editors and a breakdown of what they do:

Developmental editor: A developmental editor reviews a manuscript's structure and content for structural errors or weaknesses. They assist authors in crafting storylines, characters, and themes, as well as providing constructive criticism on areas that need improvement.

Developmental editors are essential in helping authors craft an organised and compelling narrative.

Copy editor: A copy editor oversees the technical aspects of a manuscript, such as grammar, punctuation, spelling and syntax.

They guarantee that the text is free from errors and consistent in style and tone.

Ultimately, copy editors are essential in producing an elegant and professional final product.

Line editor: Line editors focus on the individual sentences and paragraphs of a manuscript, making sure the language is crystal clear, concise, and captivating. They may suggest rewording sentences, cutting unnecessary words, or adding descriptive language to strengthen the story.

Line editors are essential in producing polished writing that works effectively.

Proofreader: Proofreaders are responsible for catching any remaining mistakes or typos in a manuscript before it's published. They review the final copy and guarantee it's free of mistakes, providing you with an error-free final product.

Editors and proofreaders are essential for producing a high-quality final product. They offer invaluable feedback and suggestions to help authors craft captivating manuscripts.

When searching for an editor and proofreader, it's essential to consider their experience, rates, and areas of specialisation. Freelance marketplaces and traditional publishing houses both provide excellent opportunities to find an editor who meets your requirements.

Some common questions about editors

Q. What is the difference between a developmental editor and copy editor?

A. A developmental editor helps shape the overall structure, pacing, and character in a manuscript, while copy editors specialise in mechanics such as grammar, spelling, and punctuation.

Q. How can I choose an editor for my manuscript?

A. Research potential editors' experience working with authors within your genre and writing level, obtain references or samples of their work, and budget accordingly for professional editing in your writing process.

Q. How much does editing typically cost?

A. Editing costs vary widely based on factors like an editor's experience, the length and complexity of your manuscript, and whether developmental editing costs more than copyediting, for example. When engaging an editor for editing work, always discuss pricing and payment before beginning work on it. Editing can cost anywhere from $100 to $1,000. But it is well worth the investment – just make sure you do your research.

Q. What is the typical length of time a writing edit usually takes?

A. Editing can last anywhere from several weeks to several months, depending on its scope and the complexity of your manuscript. Be sure to discuss deadlines and timelines with your editor before commencing editing work.

Q. What should I expect during the editing process?

A. You should anticipate receiving feedback and revision suggestions from your editor during the editing process. Being open to receiving this advice and willing to make the necessary changes for an improved manuscript is key to a smooth editing experience. Communication between the editor and client is vital for its success.

27

Book Marketing

Marketing your book correctly can mean the difference between failing to sell a single copy and becoming a bestseller in your niche. Get it right, and the world will know your name.

Here are some book marketing tips to help you succeed with your science fiction book:

Start early: Don't wait until your book has been published to begin marketing it; begin building an author platform and promoting it as soon as possible. This may include setting up a website or blog, growing social media followings, and networking within the science fiction community.

Establish a website or blog: Create a website or blog to show-case your writing and provide information about your book. Be sure to include a section about you as an author as well as ways for readers to contact you directly.

Create social media accounts: Launch accounts on popular social media platforms like Twitter, Facebook, and Instagram and use these platforms to regularly post about your writing process and excerpts from your book and to interact with fellow authors and readers in the science fiction community.

Determine your target audience: Who are you targeting? Identify the demographics, interests, and reading habits of your ideal reader to tailor marketing efforts accordingly.

Example:

Target audience: Fans of hard science fiction.

Demographics: Age 18-45, college educated, tech-savvy, and enthusiastic about science and technology.

Interests: Space exploration, artificial intelligence, futurist movements, and science news updates and developments.

Reading habits: Enjoys reading science fiction books that focus on scientific principles and futuristic technologies.

How to target marketing: Leverage social media platforms such as Twitter and Instagram to share science news related to space exploration, AI advancements, and futuristic technologies.

Discover book bloggers and bookstagrammers who specialise in reviewing hard science fiction books, and offer them free copies of your book in exchange for honest reviews.

Make time to attend science fiction conventions and events focused on science and technology to connect with potential readers for your book and promote its publication.

Utilise targeted advertising on popular social media platforms like Facebook and Instagram to reach readers who are passionate about science and technology.

Submit exclusive content such as interviews with scientists and technologists or sneak previews of scientific research related to your book's topic to engage and excite target readers and increase the excitement for its release.

Build an eye-catching book cover: Your book cover is often the first thing potential readers see; make sure it stands out and accurately represents its genre and theme.

We give you LOTS of help in our workbook: **"How To Write A Winning Fiction Book Outline - Sci-Fi Workbook."**

Here is a reminder of what to include on your science fiction novel front cover:

Opt for bold and contrasting colours: Make an impactful cover design using vibrant and eye-catching hues that capture readers' interest by using colours that stand out against each other; think about which hues represent themes and ideas within your book, then incorporate these into a cover that accurately represents it!

Use futuristic designs: Science fiction is known for featuring cutting-edge technologies and designs, so incorporate those features into your cover. Consider metallic colours, geometric shapes, or other design elements that give a futuristic feel to the cover design.

Maintain a simple design: An overly complicated or busy cover design may turn away potential readers, so keep your design clean and focused on the key elements of your story.

Gather feedback from others: Seek the opinions of friends, family, or fellow writers regarding your cover design. Consider running a poll on social media to gather opinions from your target audience.

Hire a professional designer: If your design skills don't quite measure up to expectations, consider consulting with a professional book cover designer who can create something that accurately represents your book and attracts potential readers. They'll work closely with you to design something that catches readers' eye without distracting from what the book itself says about itself.

Connect with book bloggers and bookstagrammers: Reach out to book bloggers and bookstagrammers within the science fiction community and offer them a complimentary copy of your book in exchange for an honest review. This can help generate buzz for it while broadening its reach and readership.

Here is an example email to help you with the above tip:

Dear [Bookstagrammer's Name],

As I found your bookstagram page and was inspired by its dedication to science fiction books, I would be truly honoured if you would consider reviewing my novel.

My novel is entitled [Book Title] and features interstellar travel, cutting-edge technologies, and diverse characters set in an alternate future. I believe it would make a wonderful read for your fans who share our passion for this genre.

I would be happy to provide you with a complimentary copy of my book in exchange for an honest review on any platform of your choosing. If this interests you, simply let me know which format (e-book or physical copy) and the shipping details that work best for you, and I am more than happy to address any inquiries about its content that arise.

Thank you so much for taking the time to reply, and I am looking forward to hearing back from you soon.

Regards, and best wishes from [Your Name].

Or you could try this tweet:

Calling all book bloggers and bookstagrammers! I am looking for honest reviews of my latest novel and would be happy to provide a complimentary copy in exchange. Reach out to me by DM if interested! #amwriting #bookreview #sciencefiction

Attend writing events: Attend writing events and conventions to network with fellow science fiction authors and readers, build relationships, and get your name out there. This can help create lasting bonds while increasing the visibility of your name in the science fiction community.

Offer exclusive content: Offering your readers exclusive content such as bonus chapters, behind-the-scenes footage, and short stories will help build excitement around your book and promote reader engagement with both yourself and your writing.

Try this post:

As my way of thanking readers, I'm offering exclusive content like behind-the-scenes interviews, character sketches, and more. Sign up now to my newsletter to gain access to this exciting bonus material! #scifiwriter #exclusivecontent #newsletter

Are you curious to know what inspired my latest sci-fi adventure? Check out the exclusive behind-the-scenes footage that I am sharing with my readers. Join me on my exciting journey! #amwriting #exclusivecontent #behindthescenes

Create an email list: Use Mailchimp or ConvertKit to create a landing page, offering readers free samples of chapters or short stories in exchange for their email addresses. Promote this landing page via social media channels and online communities.

By gathering the email addresses of readers interested in your book and sending out newsletters and updates via email marketing, this strategy can help build a loyal fan base while keeping readers engaged with your writing.

How to start:

Building your email list: Begin by creating a sign-up form on your website or social media accounts where readers can provide their email addresses to sign up and stay informed about your book. Alternatively, collect emails during events or through other promotional strategies.

Select an email marketing platform: There are many email marketing platforms, including Mailchimp, Constant Contact, and ConvertKit, available; select one that meets both your needs and budget requirements.

Make a newsletter template: Craft a newsletter template that reflects your brand, including information about your book, your writing process, and exclusive content. Ensure there is a call-to-action (CTA) that encourages readers to engage with it.

Regular newsletters: Consider sending regular newsletters to your email list, such as once a month or every other week. Be sure to include updates about your book, exclusive content, events or promotions that might occur, etc.

Analyse your results: Make use of your email marketing platform's analytics feature to track open rates, click-through rates, and other key metrics about newsletter readers and reader engagement. Take this data as an opportunity to enhance content quality while simultaneously increasing reader engagement with each issue of your newsletter.

Participate in online communities: Search out forums, groups, and communities related to your niche and join them. Participate in discussions while sharing updates about your book with them. Be mindful, though, not to spam or self-promote excessively.

Offer free copies: Reach out to book bloggers, reviewers, and readers through email or social media and offer them complimentary copies of your book in exchange for honest reviews.

Some writers find this a hard thing to do—to give away freebies after all the hard work and cost they might have gone to to get their book in print. But sometimes you have to speculate to accumulate, as they say, and giving away a free copy of your book will introduce you to your target audience, who may then pay money for your next book if they like your writing.

If you are really set against giving your whole novel away for free, then consider writing an additional short story or novella and presenting it for free to book bloggers as a "lead magnet" to your writing portfolio. By doing this, they can get to know your writing style and then potentially recommend your full-length novel to their audience.

Here is an example email to help you:

Subject: Free copy for an honest review

Dear [Name of Reviewer/Blogger/Reader],

I hope this email finds you well. My name is [Your Name], and I am a science fiction author. After discovering your [blog or website name], I was highly impressed with your work.

As someone who enjoys reading and reviewing science fiction novels, I would like to offer you a complimentary copy of [Book Title] in exchange for an honest review on your blog or Goodreads account.

I believe my book would be of interest to you and your readers, and I would love to hear your opinion. If so, please reach out, and I will send you a free copy in any format desired.

Thank you for taking the time to talk with me today. I look forward to hearing from you shortly.

Best regards,
[Your Name]

Run a giveaway: Use social media to host an online giveaway of your book or related merchandise. Encourage readers to spread the news of this opportunity to earn additional entries for sharing with their friends.

Attend book events: Attend book fairs, conventions, and other events related to science fiction to connect with readers and fellow authors in the science fiction community. This can help build your author platform while generating buzz for your book.

Collaborate with other authors: Reach out to other authors in your genre via social media or email and offer to cross-promote each other's books.

Use book promotion sites: Research book promotion sites like BookBub, BookGorilla, and Bargain Booksy and apply for free or low-cost options.

Request reviews: Reach out to friends, family, and colleagues via email or social media and invite them to leave reviews on Goodreads. Don't incentivise or pressure them into leaving positive reviews; rather, simply ask for their opinion.

Create a book trailer: Use free video editing software such as iMovie or Windows Movie Maker to craft an engaging book trailer with images, music, and text. Share the trailer on social media channels and your website for maximum exposure.

Contact local media: Explore local newspapers, radio stations, and TV stations and reach out to see if they would be interested in featuring or interviewing you for your book. Have a polished pitch ready.

Here is an example email to help you:

Subject: Request for a book review, feature, or interview

Dear [Name of contact person],

Hello, my name is [Your Name], and I am a science fiction author. I am reaching out to you because I think your readers, listeners, or viewers would be interested in hearing about my new book, [Book Title].

[Contain a brief overview of your book, such as its genre, and an outline with one or two sentences about the plot.]

I'm thrilled to share my book with the local community, and I was wondering if you would be interested in featuring it in your publication or show. Alternatively, I would be delighted to participate in an interview where we can discuss my book and its creation process.

I have attached a press release and author bio for your reference, as well as a complimentary copy of my book in case you would like to review it before the feature or interview. I would be more than happy to provide any additional information or answer any questions you may have.

Thank you for taking the time to respond. I look forward to hearing from you shortly.

Best wishes,
[Your Name]

Use author pages: Create an author page and fill it with your book's details, images, and bio. Use the page to promote your book and connect with readers.

Connect with book clubs: Research book clubs in your area or online and reach out to organisers to join discussions about your book. Be respectful and accepting of different opinions.

28

Science Fiction Writing Glossary

A - Alien: Any creature from another planet or galaxy depicted with distinctive physical features and abilities that are usually shown to originate from distant areas.

Artificial Intelligence (AI): Artificial intelligence refers to any programme or machine designed to simulate human intelligence and perform tasks without direct human input.

Black holes: Areas in space where gravitational forces are so powerful that nothing—not even light—can escape their gravitational pull.

Clones: DNA copies created artificially that replicate all aspects of an organism's genes.

Cyborg: Cyborgs are beings that combine human and machine components, typically possessing enhanced abilities that exceed those of normal people.

Dystopian society/world: An imaginary future society where oppressive or authoritarian conditions prevail.

Extraterrestrial: Anything located beyond Earth or its atmosphere, whether living or nonliving.

FTL: Faster-than-light technology. In science fiction, this term describes travel or communication that occurs faster than light speed.

Galaxy: An immense system composed of stars, dust, and gas held together by gravity.

Hologram: An object created using lasers or other technologies that projects three-dimensional images onto surfaces in three dimensions.

Intergalactic: Pertaining to or taking place between galaxies.

Jump drive (formerly "Loop drive"): This is a fictional propulsion system which allows spaceships to travel faster than light by jumping directly to another point in space-time.

Kaiju: This is a Japanese term used to refer to giant monsters frequently depicted in science fiction and monster movie cinematic works.

Laser: An instrument that emits a highly focused beam of light that can be used for cutting, welding, or other tasks.

Martian: Any individual or object native to Mars.

Nanotechnology: This refers to the use of microscopic machines or materials for creating new products or devices.

Orbit: An orbit is defined as an object travelling around another object in space, such as when a planet orbits a star.

Portal: An imaginary device or concept that provides for instantaneous travel between two points in space or time.

Quantum: Relating to or related to quantum mechanics, which is an area of physics that examines particle behaviour at subatomic levels.

Robot: An autonomous machine designed to carry out specific tasks without human assistance.

Spaceship: An aircraft specifically designed to travel into space. They may transport people and goods between planets or galaxies.

Time travel: Time travel is a fictional concept involving travelling back in time to different eras or events, often through time machines.

UFO (Unidentified Flying Object): Any unknown flying object often associated with extraterrestrial life or advanced technology.

Virtual reality: A computer-generated environment that simulates realistic experiences or situations.

Warp drive: An imaginary propulsion system that allows spaceships to travel faster than light by distorting space-time and travelling at increased speed.

Xenobiology: The study of alien life and biology.

Yoda: Yoda is an iconic character from Star Wars known for his wisdom and distinctive speaking style.

Zero gravity (ZGV): This refers to conditions in which there appears to be no gravitational force acting upon an object, often experienced during orbital flight or free fall.

Conclusion

Congratulations! You've reached the end of this book and hopefully gained valuable insights and techniques that can help you write an unforgettable novel in this genre.

Through this book, we have discussed all of the components that comprise an effective science fiction tale. We addressed how important it is to create engaging characters who resonate with readers, with clear motivations and flaws that propel the plot forward.

We discussed the crucial role that plot twists, red herrings, and suspense play in keeping readers interested from page one of your novel. Furthermore, we explored using descriptive language, metaphors, and imagery to build a world readers can get lost in.

We emphasised the significance of crafting an eye-catching book cover that accurately represents your story and appeals to its target audience and explored various marketing strategies, such as creating an author platform, reaching out to book bloggers/bookstagrammers for endorsement, and using email marketing to promote your book.

Finally, we examined the three-act structure, which can assist you in creating an engaging reading experience for your audience and mapping out a clear conflict-resolution relationship within your story.

By following these guidelines, you're sure to write an impressive science fiction novel that will enthral readers. Science fiction allows writers to explore all kinds of possibilities - don't be intimidated by its vast possibilities!

Thank you for joining us on this adventure through science fiction writing!

We wish you every success on your writing journey and look forward to witnessing all the remarkable stories that emerge from it.

What now?

Now that you're equipped with the knowledge and tools to write your very own page-turning science fiction novel, it's time to take action and make it happen!

Our **"How To Write A Winning Fiction Book Outline - Sci-Fi Workbook"** provides all the resources and guidance you need to bring your book to life with ease and enjoyment.

With our done-for-you novel outline templates and prompts, you can create a captivating story from scratch. We'll guide you through every step of the process, from planning and writing, to publishing and beyond.

Imagine holding your book in your hands, knowing that readers are eagerly waiting to devour your story. With our winning strategy and your unique ideas, success is within reach.

And the best part? You can make money while you sleep, as your book reaches readers around the world.

Our workbook is the tool you wish you had from the beginning, providing all the resources and guidance you need to turn your ink into income. So what are you waiting for?

Grab your copy of **"How To Write A Winning Fiction Book**

Outline - Sci-Fi Workbook" now and let us help you take your writing to the next level.

Your readers are waiting for your amazing story, and we're here to help you make it happen – every step of the way.

Vicky & Claire

HackneyandJones.com

www.ingramcontent.com/pod-product-compliance
Lightning Source LLC
Chambersburg PA
CBHW071322150726
47997CB00002B/574